WORDS with
PICTURES

WORDS with PICTURES

Welsh Images and Images of Wales
in the Popular Press, 1640-1860

Peter Lord

PLANET

First published in Wales in 1995 by
Planet
PO Box 44
Aberystwyth
Dyfed
Cymru/Wales

ISBN 0 9505188 2 4

Designed by Peter Lord and Glyn Rees
Printed by Gwasg Gomer, Llandysul, Dyfed

Published with the financial support of the
Foundation for Sport and the Arts

Contents

Foreword

As well as the interaction of words and pictures, this book is about the interaction of two cultures. In the period under consideration, the Welsh language was dominant in Welsh culture, so much of the material has had to be translated. I've given priority to rendering the spirit and the rhythm of the ballads, since these seem to me to be their essential qualities, even when, on occasions, this has meant deviating from close equivalents of meaning for every word. Some of the more formal verses are given in literal translation only, since the complexities of their alliteration are almost impossible to render in English. All the quoted poems and texts are given in the original for Welsh-speaking readers, while Welsh titles are translated into English when first mentioned unless the context makes their meaning obvious. I must take responsibility for any misinterpretations of the sometimes obscure references and eccentric spellings of the originals.

I would like to thank the Literature Committee of the Arts Council of Wales for funding a period of research which enabled me to complete the text, and the Foundation for Sport and the Arts for the grant which has enabled *Planet* to publish the book. The staff of the National Library of Wales were generous with their time and expertise, both during the research and in preparing the bulk of the reproductions in the book. Finally, I would like to thank John Barnie and Helle Michelsen of *Planet* for their enthusiastic support of the project and their advice on the text, and Glyn Rees for his design.

Cerddaist mewn blwyddyn
Y mynydd a'r dyffryn:
Tramwyaist bob adwy
O fôn i fynnwy.
Eist fel oen diniwed
I gorlan y defed:
Cefaist yno'n ebrwydd
Orphwys a chynhesrwydd:
Y Bobl ddifales
A'th roent yn eu mynwes;
A'r diniwed gwirion
A'th roent wrth eu dwyfron...

1 Words, pictures and the people

Printed pictures are almost as old as the printed word. The earliest means of reproduction was the woodcut, the same process by which the type itself was made. The first blocks may well have been cut by the printers themselves, but specialisms in the manufacture of presses, type and pictures soon developed. Nevertheless, in Wales as late as about 1813, the printer John Jones of Trefriw built his own new press and cast his own type.[1] Pictures in the popular press developed characteristic forms in various parts of Europe. In France, in the tradition known as *Imagerie*, the woodcut remained the primary medium into the nineteenth century, although engravings on copper and lithographs are also encompassed by the term. In England, the combination of ballads and broadsides with a woodcut on the title page (and sometimes in the text as well), characterised the popular press. By the early seventeenth century it had become a conventional form. Indeed, in 1648, the London news pamphlet *Mercurius Britanicus Alive Again* asked "How many Ballads would sell without a formal woodcut?" The comment, presumably intended as a slight on the literary quality of the accompanying texts, confirms that for many of the public, the availability of cheap pictures was just as important as having something amusing, improving or scandalous to read, or to have read to them if they were not literate themselves. Pictures are explicit and immediate in comparison to words which are a more laborious code. If a single event or situation contains the focal idea then a picture is an ideal medium. The word is better at consequences and implications. The combination of the two, in various proportions, provides the sharpest focus possible and the essence of the popular press.

Initially, the popular press was an urban phenomenon. The intense and crowded atmosphere of the town provided both the best environment for generating the subject matter and also enough potential customers to make a profit for the producer. In the seventeenth and early eighteenth centuries, Wales must have seemed a most unpromising market. Among a disparate population, there was little sense of common focus that might generate attractive subject matter. In any case, the Licensing Act made printing illegal outside London, Oxford and Cambridge, until 1695.

The earliest successful attempt to overcome these difficulties was made by Thomas Jones, known as Thomas Jones yr Almanaciwr, who published the first of his series of 32 Welsh-language almanacks in London in 1679. Unlike his English counterparts, Thomas Jones had to transport his publications to a potential audience, much smaller in total than the population of London alone, spread thinly over a country 200 miles away.[2] With prodigious energy, he developed a system of distributors in the small towns, from where his products were sent on again for sale at fairs and markets in the villages by itinerant pedlars and perhaps by ballad singers. His success over such a long period, not only in selling his products at the main market towns near the border, but in ensuring that they arrived in the homes of ordinary people in the remotest corners of the countryside, was remarkable. In the almanack for 1693, he addressed his own publication:

> Wandering, through the year
> Deep valley, mountain sheer,
> River, plain and sea,
> From Môn to Mynwy.
> As a lamb, innocent,
> To the sheep-fold you went:
> There, soon, you were given
> Warmth and safe haven:
> The people, simple, kind,
> Took you, with heart and mind:
> And the innocent truth
> You set before them...

For Thomas Jones the popular press was a patriotic mission as well as a money-making enterprise. His work was the more remarkable since it was undertaken before the English fashion for the idea of Ancient Britain gave Welsh intellectuals new self-confidence in the middle of the eighteenth

Formschneider (wood engraver), by Jost Amman, 1564.

Printing Press, built by John Jones about 1813.

Imagerie—a seller of religious prints in France, late 18th century.

9

Byddent yn canu yn y ffeiriau mewn pellter priodol oddiwrth eu gilydd, a chylch o ieuenctyd yn gwasgu o'u cwmpas, ac ambell i ffarmwr yn gwrando'n ddifyr yn eu plith. Gan eu bod yn canu cymaint yn yr awyr agored yr oedd eu lleisiau braidd yn afrywiog, ond byddent yn dyweyd y geiriau yn eglur, yn acenu yn gywir, ac yn rhoddi ei sain briodol i bob llythyren. Golwg braidd yn slyfenllyd oedd ar Dic, ond yr oedd Owen yn ei got lwyd beth yn fwy gweddus, a chanddo fantais ar Dic am fod ei olwg ganddo, ac yr oedd yn gwneyd y defnydd goreu o hono, gan dremio yn llygaid y llanciau a'r morwynion gyda gwên hudolus a chwareus, a'r lluaws yn gwasgu ato gan estyn eu dwylaw am y gerdd...

Aberystwyth Fair, by Samuel Ireland, 1797.

century and the first glimmerings of the idea that Wales might again be home to a living culture began to appear. The work of Thomas Jones certainly played an important part in developing literacy and a potential market for the increasing amount of material which became available as a consequence of the eighteenth-century revival.[3]

In his almanacks, Thomas Jones gave some indication of the first level of the distribution system he created when he named a number of individuals involved in the work in border towns. However, little is known of the distribution of the almanacks further down the line, or of the distribution of the ballads and broadsides which were printed in substantial numbers for the Welsh market from the 1720s in Chester and Shrewsbury. All the first-hand accounts of pedlars of popular literature date from the nineteenth century, and nearly all concern ballad singers. They are retrospective accounts, and consequently picturesque, and concentrate almost exclusively on the performance. They are singularly uninformative about the nuts and bolts of the production and distribution of printed ballads. In his description of Ywain Meirion and Dic Dywyll as he remembered them in the 1840s, Richard Jones Owen, Glaslyn said:

"They would sing at the fairs at a respectful distance from each other, a circle of young people pressing around and an occasional farmer listening, amused, amongst them. Because they sang so much in the open air their voices were rather harsh, but they would pronounce the words clearly, with correct stress and giving a proper sound to each letter. Dic was rather slovenly looking, but Owen in his grey coat was somewhat more respectable, and he had the advantage over Dic because he could see, and he would make the best use of it, fixing the eyes of the young men and women with a bewitching and playful smile, the throng pressing towards him and stretching out their hands for the song..."[4]

Yr oedd ei het yn dolciog, ac yn debyg i hen het silc wedi bod mewn brwydrau lawer, a llinyn neu ddau o amgylch ei choryn, a rhes o gerddi o dan y ddau linyn, wedi eu sicrhau yn ofalus rhag i'r gwynt eu dwyn. Ac yn ei law byddai ffon hir gyda bagl fawr ar ei phen, a phan yn canu yn y ffair, gosodai y ffon o'i flaen yn gyffelyb i'r Datgeiniaid Penpasdwn gynt, a phwysai ei ddwy law ar fagl ei ffon; yn y llaw chwith, byddai ganddo swp o gerddi, ac yn ei law dde byddai ganddo un gerdd, a phan yn canu, byddai yn estyn y gerdd hono ar y ffon, tua chyfeiriad y gwrandawyr, fel i ofyn iddynt ei phrynu.

Mewn perthynas i Owain Meirion, 'roeddwn yn siarad am dano yn ddiweddar gyda chyfaill, yr hwn a'm hadgoffai fod yr hen fachgen yn arfer gwisgo het uchel, yn yr hon y cariai ei faledau. Un tro yr oedd wedi cael *lift* mewn cerbyd yn ymyl y Cann Office yn sir Drefaldwyn, ac oblegid i'r cerbyd gychwyn yn bur sydyn, syrthiodd yr het oddiar ei ben, a gwasgarwyd y baledau ar hyd y ffordd...

About the same time, Richard Williams also remembered Ywain Meirion:

"With regard to Owain Meirion, I was talking about him not long ago to a friend who reminded me that the old boy used to wear a high hat in which he carried his ballads. One day he got a lift in a cart near Cann Office in Montgomeryshire but when the cart started rather suddenly, his hat fell off his head and all the ballads were scattered in the road..."[5]

When Ellis Owen Ellis drew a cartoon for *Y Punch Cymraeg* in 1858, satirising both the proverbial mistakes made in the almanacks and the gullibility of the audience, he chose Ywain Meirion as his subject, on his way to Ffair y Borth. Robert Griffith, writing in 1910, remembered Ywain Meirion much like this, with his "dented hat, like an old silk hat that had seen many battles, with one or two black bands around the crown and a row of songs under the bands carefully secured against the wind blowing them away. And in his hand would be a long staff with a big crooked head, and when he sang at the fair he would hold the staff out in front of him like the old *Datgeiniaid Penpasdwn*, and press both hands on the crook at the top; in his left hand would be a bundle of songs and in his right hand he would hold just one, and while he was singing he would pass that song out towards his audience on the staff, as if to ask them to buy."[6]

In the 1780s, Moses Griffith painted a miniature portrait of a *datgeiniad penpasdwn* for his patron Thomas Pennant's description of the Eisteddfod tradition. The ragged *datgeiniad*, "lowest of the musical tribe"[7] according to Pennant, accords closely with Robert Griffith's description of Ywain Meirion, and indicates that, despite a superficial similarity, the Welsh ballad singer and the English equivalent were very different phenomena. The Welsh ballad singer was heir to an ancient tradition of profesional poets. The medieval tradition of the *datgeiniad*, who even if of a low grade was nevertheless a professional poet and musician with a knowledge of the

Cyhoeddwyr anturiaethus yn wynebu tua "Ffair y Borth", by Ellis Owen Ellis, 1858.

Datceiniad Penpasdwn, by Moses Griffith, c.1778.

11

POWYS ESTEIDDFOD
Sep 1825.

Roedd ganddo glamp o bawl
A darlun rhyfel Russia
Fe roddai anferth fawl
I rengoedd y Crimea.

Canu mewn cylch,
Eisteddfod Powys, 1824,
by an unknown engraver.

Abel Jones, Bardd Crwst,
by John Thomas, c.1870.

classical forms and the ability to play harp or crwth, was a part of the consciousness of Ywain Meirion and his contemporaries. This consciousness was manifested to some extent in the content of the ballads and also in their form. Ywain certainly made use of *cynghanedd,*[8] knew the work of some classical poets including Siôn Phylip and Edmwnd Prys, and sang to the harp at *eisteddfodau,* as well as in the streets. He was among the competitors at the Dyfed Eisteddfod of 1824. An engraving of the following year's proceedings in Powys, showing a group of ragged competitors, is one of the very few contemporary visual records of such people. They are probably competing at *canu mewn cylch,* in which each competitor in turn had to remember a verse of a poem which had been chosen by the harper and was sung to his accompaniment. Competitors were eliminated one by one if they were unable to recall the next verse. Ywain may be among them, but no photograph of him survives from his old age to assist in the identification. Despite their linear connection to a great tradition, as Tegwyn Jones has pointed out in his study of Ywain Meirion,[9] the ballad singers were "*pobl yr ymylon*"—people on the margin—and while the tradition was alive John Thomas was the only photographer who interested himself in documenting the poor, the homeless and the itinerant. The old people in his photographs of the 1860s and 1870s, their faces distorted by life-long poverty, are those who in their youth crowded around the ballad singers at the fairs, described by Glaslyn. John Thomas took the only formal portrait to survive of a nineteenth-century ballad singer, Abel Jones, Bardd Crwst, offering a ballad with one hand and holding the penny he has received for it in the other.

The written descriptions of those who remembered Bardd Crwst, Ywain Meirion, Dic Dywyll and others in their prime, make almost no reference to the role of pictures in their business. However, in 1855, in a poem describing Ywain Meirion, Howell Rowlands included a verse to the

following effect:

> He had a staff full five feet long
> And the war in Russia's pictures;
> He praised them loud in grateful song
> Crimea's noble victors.[10]

No printed version of Ywain's ballad about the war survives with an illustration, so it seems most likely that he was displaying, pasted to a board, a wood engraving cut from the *Illustrated London News* or a similar magazine. The same magazine might have been the source of the information relayed in the ballad. The Battle of Alma, portrayed in *Cassell's Illustrated Family Paper* would have been a good choice with particular Welsh interest. The death of Captain Wynn at Alma, during the siege of Sebastopol, became celebrated enough to be listed among the set topics for the painting competition at the Llangollen Eisteddfod three years later, in 1858.

Nineteenth-century observers were equally uninformative on the relationship between the ballad writers, singers and illustrators and their printers. On eighteenth-century ballads, imprints such as "Elizabeth Adams dros (on behalf of) William Davies", are common, showing that the instigator—sometimes the author, sometimes the distributor—was Welsh but the printer English. This suggests that the difficulties of marketing made an entrepreneurial attitude on the part of printers unusual. They might have turned themselves into publishers by financing the printing themselves, but most did not. Thomas Jones yr Almanaciwr worked in this way, but he was exceptional, and motivated, as we have seen, not simply by profit but also by patriotism. Despite the dominant position of the Trefriw printer, John Jones, in the production of ballads through the first half of the nineteenth century, the evidence of his account books makes it clear that the instigation and capitalisation of a significant part of his output, even after he moved to Llanrwst and hugely expanded his business, came from authors and illustrators. The engraver and portrait painter Hugh Hughes, for instance, had John Jones print his illustrated sheet *Trioedd y Gwragedd* (The Women's Triads) in 1821. Hughes wrote the *Trioedd*, engraved two blocks for it, paid for the printing and distributed it himself, a substantial undertaking. He cannot have expected to make any money and may well have given the sheets away as he toured the country drawing for his up-market volume of wood engravings, *The Beauties of Cambria*. Hughes was motivated largely by his mission to use popular

13

John Jones, Llanrwst, by an unknown photographer, c. 1860-65.

texts and pictures to enlighten and exhort the people.

Itinerant portrait painters like Hughes and William Roos were in close contact with popular poets who sometimes, like them, travelled up and down Wales selling their wares. At Christmas, 1844, Roos met Hugh Derfel at Llangollen. The poet was returning north having toured the country selling copies of his book, *Blodeu'r Gân* (The Flowers of Poesy). Roos was working his way south, painting portraits, and was much taken with Hugh Derfel's poem *Y Cyfamod Disigl.* "I have read many times your verses on the Steadfast Covenant," he said. "I have to admit that these have had much moralising effect on me—if I had listened to a hundred sermons they would not have had so much effect on me."[11] His taste proved consistent with popular opinion at large—the poem became Hugh Derfel's most famous work and a popular text on ballad sheets for many years.

In 1826, with less complex motives than Hugh Hughes, one W. Brooks had John Jones print a title page and bind together 23 ballads (not all originally printed by him) to sell under the collective name *Piser Alis* (Alice's Pitcher). Brooks, as far as is known, was simply an itinerant seller of popular literature, trying to make a living. Such individuals were not always reliable in the payment of bills, their ability to do so reflecting the vagaries of the market. In 1854, John Jones wrote to his son Evan, also a printer:

"You won't profit much from dealing with Owen James—the old boy's a lying hypocrite. Unless the ballads sell as he expects, he'll never come for them, nor pay for those he's had. I've printed a thousand of Edward Jones, Maes y Plwm's *Cerddi Swyngyfaredd* (Poems of Enchantment) for him. He came with no money to get a hundred of them, and that was months ago—and I don't suppose I'll ever see him again."[12]

In a letter sent to Evan the previous week, John Jones gave an idea of the substantial quantity of popular material regularly dispatched from his office in Llanrwst to more dependable distributors:

14

Ni fyddi di fawr yn dy fantais o ddelio ag Owen James,—hen ragrithiwr celwyddog yw yr hen greadur. Oni werth y cerddi yn ol ei ddisgwyliad, ni ddaw efe byth ar eu cyfwl, nag i dalu am a gafodd. Yr wyf fi wedi argraffu mil iddo o Gerddi Swyngyfaredd, gan Edward Jones, Maes y Plwm. Daeth i geisio un cant ohonynt heb arian, a hyny ers misoedd yn ol, · a thebyg na welaf mo hono mwy.

Y mae genym... 1400 o Almanaciau wedi eu pacio ynghyd a 100 Dyddiadur, 60 Telyn Aur, ac o gylch 2000 o gerddi bach —ac yr ydym yn disgwyl Carrier Ffestiniog yma heno.

Yr wyf gwedi darllen llawer gwaith eich penillion ar y Cyfamod Disigl. Mae yn gorfod i mi addef i fod y rhai hyn gwedi moesoli llawer arnai—pe buaswn yn gwrandaw cant o bregethai ni wnaethant gymaint o effaith arnaf.

O ddiffyg llwybr effeithiol i wneyd cyhoeddiad y gwaith yn hysbys yn fwy cyffredinol, ac i ddanfon y llyfrau yn fwy cyson i'r ardaloedd lle y mae syched am eu cael, a bod o herwydd hyny lawer o'r rhai a argraffwyd yn sefyll ar law; bernir yn angenrheidiol oedi'r Cyhoeddiad dros ychydig, gan olygu yn y cyfamser arfer moddion i symud y rhwystrau a enwyd...

"I've got... 1400 Almanacs packed and a hundred Diaries, 60 *Telyn Aur*, and about 2000 small ballads—and I'm expecting the carrier from Ffestiniog here tonight."

Hugh Hughes, by William Williams, ab Caledfryn, 1894

The names of Ywain Meirion and other ballad singers and writers appear as entrepreneurs on ballads printed all over Wales, in the same way that Hugh Hughes financed *Trioedd y Gwragedd*. In the 1830s, when John Jones began to print substantial numbers of large illustrated sheets, the name of James Cope, his finest illustrator, also sometimes appeared as entrepreneur as well as engraver. Nevertheless, John Jones certainly printed sheets on his own account as well. He kept in his possession wood blocks cut both by Hughes and by Cope but it seems highly unlikely that he paid the engravers (or the writers) any royalty when he reprinted their work for his own benefit over very many years.

The relationship between John Jones and Hugh Hughes, along with that established between the artist and the printer John Evans in Carmarthen, was crucial for the development of illustration in popular Welsh-language publications. Hughes was the link between the illustrative tradition of the English popular press and an emergent Welsh voice. Although he did not produce blocks especially to illustrate Welsh ballad sheets, Hughes was responsible for almost all the earliest popular book illustrations and for the first regular use of illustrations in periodicals. Nevertheless, several of his pioneering ventures in the field, notably *Yr Addysgydd* (The Educator) with John Evans in 1823, and even as late as 1836 and *Y Papyr Newydd Cymraeg*, the first weekly Welsh-language newspaper, were afflicted by the old problems of distribution which had held things back so long. In the last issue of *Yr Addysgydd*, the earliest original Welsh-language children's periodical to contain pictures, the editors commented:

"For the want of an effective means to make the publication of the work more generally known and to send the books more regularly to the areas where there is a demand for them, resulting in many that have been printed being left on the shelf, it has been deemed necessary to interrupt the publication for a little while; the intention, in the meantime is to find a way of removing the above obstacles."[13]

Unlike letters, pictures cannot be reconstituted to tell other stories except in the most generalised way, so that each image, produced for a particular

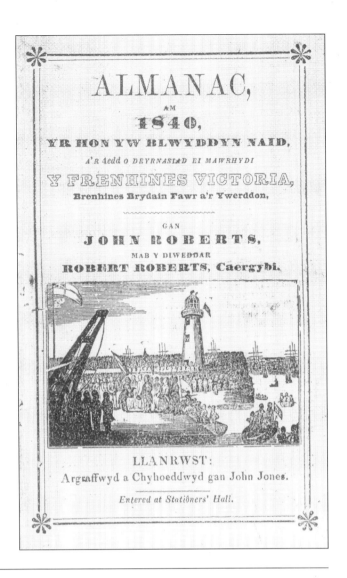

ALMANAC,
AM
1840,
YR HON YW BLWYDDYN NAID,
A'R 4edd O DEYRNASIAD EI MAWRHYDI
Y FRENHINES VICTORIA,
Brenhines Brydain Fawr a'r Ywerddon,
GAN
JOHN ROBERTS,
MAB Y DIWEDDAR
ROBERT ROBERTS, Caergybi.

LLANRWST:
Argraffwyd a Chyhoeddwyd gan John Jones.

Entered at Stationers' Hall.

Almanac am 1840,
written by John Roberts
and published by John
Jones, Llanrwst. Wood
engraving by Hugh
Hughes, 1821.

text, would have become redundant after a single use had it not become an accepted practice to use the old blocks again and again in association with texts to which they were not relevant. John Jones enlivened the cover of John Roberts's almanack for 1840 by reprinting a small view of the landing of George IV at Holyhead, cut by Hugh Hughes in 1821, for instance. As a consequence of this practice, the vast majority of surviving woodcuts from the seventeenth and eighteenth centuries are not known in the context of their original texts. When a printer went bankrupt or died, the blocks were sold with the type and stayed in circulation for many years. Old and worn out blocks were often replaced by copies not to fit particular texts but simply because they were popular. The market for prints was very conservative in its tastes. In the 1820s, Batchelar, the London publisher of broadsides, refused to sell his old blocks even when offered new and better ones to replace them. "Yes," he said, "but better are not so good; I can get better myself; now these are old favourites, and better cuts will not please my customers so well!"[14] That this convention of recycling was not only acceptable, but a delight to the audience, is testimony to the value put on the image for itself alone, rather than as illustration.

Many ballads and broadsides probably ended up pasted or pinned to the wall, and to meet this specific demand for pictures, publishers of chapbooks also produced single sheet prints on which the image was clearly the dominant element. Some of this seventeenth and eighteenth-century English material concerned Wales, such as the woodcut image of Poor Taff, riding on a goat, which was still being issued in the late 1740s. A copy of this popular image, significantly cut out from its text, is accurately depicted, pinned to the cottage wall, in the background of *The Welch Curate*, an intaglio engraving probably published in the 1770s. Although it is clearly meant to define the Welshness of the curate who is the main subject of the print, there is no reason to doubt that it is also a realistic

16

The Welch Curate, detail,
published by Bowles and
Carver, London, c.1770.

depiction of the way popular images were used. Such views of the insides of the houses of ordinary people in the seventeenth and eighteenth centuries are rare, so that it is difficult to determine just how commonly pictures were used in this way as the poor people's equivalent of the oil paintings of the rich. After a period in decline, the woodcut achieved great popularity again in the early nineteenth century primarily as a visual form, pioneered in London by Catnach and Pitts but soon developed in Wales on the large format sheets produced by John Jones and by Isaac Thomas in Cardigan. Unfortunately, by the time that photography was sufficiently developed to record the dark interiors of the houses of ordinary people, the tradition was dying. Nevertheless, wood engravings cut from illustrated newspapers—the descendants of the woodcut prints on the ballads and broadsides—appear stuck on the walls of a lead miners' barracks photographed in mid-Wales at the beginning of the twentieth century, and the inside of a croft, photographed a little earlier, has large popular prints of patriotic Scottish subjects pinned to the walls. The popular press penetrated the rural areas most remote from the towns where it originated.

Very early in the study of popular culture it became commonplace to regard the ballad and the broadside as the record of the voice of the people, as distinct from the voice of the establishment or the intelligentsia. The seventeenth-century English collector of ballads, John Selden, famously remarked that "More solid things do not show the complexion of the times so well as ballads and libels". This view has been very persistent. In a book written in 1946, popular visual culture was defined as "the art which ordinary people have, from time immemorial, introduced into their everyday lives... imposing their own tastes on the products of the craftsmen or the machine," a remark which tends—like many subsequent observations in the same vein—to imply that the people had a pre-existing and coherent taste, creating a market to which the maker simply moulded

Lead Miner's Barracks, mid-Wales, by an unknown photographer, 1901.

the product.[15] In 1980, Tegwyn Jones remarked:

"The reactions of the ballad singer to the events and developments of the day were also the reactions of his audience. In order to earn his daily bread it was necessary for him to aim at satisfactory sales and it would not pay him to take a view which was contrary to the general opinion. For those who would know the reaction of the ordinary man to the coming of the railways, to the Chartist disturbances in Newport, to the wars of the day and the hard times and shortages that came in their wake, the ballads of Ywain Meirion and others are a source of the greatest importance."[16]

Nevertheless, simply to say that popular literature and popular art were the voice of the people is to imply that they reflected life as a sort of neutral mirror. Furthermore, it implies that they reflected a single image—in other words, that the people were homogeneous and spoke with one voice. Beyond being a vehicle for the transmission into the modern world of some traditional stories and beliefs, and a confirmation of the prurient interest of the people in any age and place in scandal, disaster and crime, neither of these closely related implications is born out by the evidence. The ideas of the people were always diverse and evolving and the ballads were not infrequently inconsistent with the opinions of large numbers of them.

At the beginning of the twentieth century, Glaslyn observed, with an important difference of emphasis from the simplistic conventional wisdom, that "the things that are remembered and sung by the people

give direction to their lives and form their characters." He tells us that the ballads created public opinion rather than reflected it. Glaslyn was born in 1831, and, as we have seen, was in a position to speak of these things with some authority since he remembered the last of the itinerant ballad singers, with their roots deep in the eighteenth century:

Croft in Scotland, by an unknown photographer, c. 1900.

"There was a lot of singing and selling songs went on in the fairs at that time, and I well remember the pleasure I had in following one of the local farmers to the fairs of Eifionydd and Ardudwy as a cow boy, and how I and the rest of us would be sure to fill our pockets with new songs, and the learning and the singing of them over and over in the following weeks. Dic Dywyll and Owen Meirion were in their prime at that time, if they can be said ever to have had a prime. Anyway, they were the two most public figures in Gwynedd in the minds of the people..."[17]

Ywain Meirion and Dic Dywyll were public figures rather in the way that a television current affairs commentator is a public figure today. Ballads were seldom, themselves, first hand accounts of events, but rather passed on to the people the wisdom of newspapers and pamphlets. They were often, therefore, reflections of intellectual opinion. Glaslyn recognised that the ballads and popular visual imagery were an active force in the evolution of opinion—a part of the cultural process. To regard the material simply as a mirror of the process is an entirely retrospective perception, a historian's convenience.

DOETHINEB CENEDL Y CYMRY.

TRIOEDD Y GWRAGEDD.

TAIR rhagorgamp benyw: addfwynder, diweirdeb, a gloyw lander yn ei gorchwyl a'i gwisg.

AM dri pheth y cerir benyw: harddwch corphorol, serchogrwydd meddwl, a threfnusder teuluaidd.

TRI pheth canmoladwy ar fenyw: gwylder ymarwedd, cynildeb llaw ac amcan, a diwydrwydd teuluaidd.

TRI pheth hawddgar ar ferch: addfwyn o ddefawd, gwisg drefnus-loyw, a llafar serchogaidd.

TRI pheth molianus ar fenyw: caru bod yn nghartref, na bo yn rhy lafargar, a bod yn drugarog tu ag at a'i gofyno, sef wrth dlawd, claf, a dieithr.

TAIR dyledswydd gartrefawl benyw: gofal trefnus am ei thŷ a'i thylwyth, bod yn roesawgar wrth ei westeion, a bod yn garedig i'w gwr.

TRI pheth dwyfawl ar ferch: bod yn faddeugar, yn elusengar, ac yn anfoethus.

TRI pheth a ddanghosant wraig dda: ei gwr yn lân a threfnus ei wisg, dwyn ei phlant ar wybodau bonheddig, a bod gair da iddi gan ei chymydogion.

TRI pheth a wnant wr yn foddlon i'w wraig: glan a chyfan yn ei gwisg, serchog ei hymddwyn, a threfnus 'n lân yn ei thŷ.

TAIR arwydd gwraig ddrwg: bostio ei gweithred ei hunan, beio ar ei chymydogesau, ac ymddynu am y trechaf.

TRI pheth a ddengys ddoethineb gwraig: ei gweinyddesi yn aros yn hir yn ei gwasanaeth, ei gwr yn caru bod gartref, a borender ei theulu.

TRI pheth anferth ar forwynferch: bod yn dra chwerthingar, yn dra chwedleugar, ac yn dra sengar.

TRI gotynion benyw: bwyd, gwisgoedd, a charedigrwydd.

TRI anrhydedd gwraig: ei thŷ yn lân ac yn drefnus, ei gwr yn llwyddianus, a'i phlant yn wybodus.

TRI pheth y dylai pôb gwr eu gwneuthur tu ag at ei wraig: ei charu'n ddidwyll, ei chynnal yn ddiddiffyg yn ol y byd a fo arno, a gadael iddi ym mhob peth a berthyn i drefn ei thŷ, ei thylwyth, a'i gorchwyl.

TRI pheth y dylai meibion eu gwneuthur tu ag at y merched: ymgyfeillach garedig, anrhegion gweddeiddbarch, ac ymddwyn syberwydbwyll.

TRI pheth a wedd i'r merched tu ag at y meibion: gwylder serchogaidd, caredigrwydd parodbwyll, a syberwyd benywaidd gweddeiddbarch.

TRI pheth a barant i wraig gael tybied yn dda am dani: ei gwr a'i phlant yn lân olchedig eu dillad, ei dodrefn yn lân a threfnus, a'i bod yn ymgadw gartref.

TRI pheth a ddangosant wraig yn anniwair: bod yn chwerthingar heb wybod pa'm, yn falch ar ei phryd a'i gwedd, ac yn achwyngar ar ei gwr.

TRI pheth hoffaidd gan wr eu gweled ar ei wraig: ei bod

TRI pheth ffeiddfrwnt ar wraig: aflendid corph a dodrefn, sengarwch a dioglydrwydd.

yn rhinweddus, yn cadw ei thŷ yn drefnus, ac yn ei gorchwyl yn fedrus.

TRI pheth a wnant wr yn anghenus: tylwyth gwallus, gwraig foethus, ac yntau yn afradus.

TRI pheth anghysurus i wr fod hebddynt: tân yn ei aelwyd, arian yn ei bwrs, a'i wraig yn ei wely.

TRI pheth a wnant wr yn foddlon i'w giniaw: ei gylla yn iachus, ei fwyd yn flasus, a'i wraig yn fedrus.

TRI pheth a wnant wr yn llon ei wynebpryd: ei dir yn dirion, ei berllan yn ffrwythlon, a'i wraig yn rhadlon.

TRI pheth anesmwyth i wr yn ei dŷ: ei ffumer yn mygu, ei gronglwyd yn dyferu, a'i wraig yn ymdaeru.

TRI pheth a wnant wr yn hawddfydig: ei dŷ yn llawn, ei wraig yn syber, ei blant yn brydferth ar gorph a meddwl.

TRI pheth a barant i wr hoffi cartref: ei deulu yn ddiosparthus, ei orchwylion yn llwyddianus, a'i wraig yn gariadus.

TRI pheth y dylai gwraig briod eu caru uwchlaw pob peth arall yn hyn o fyd: ei gwr, ei phlant, a'i chartref.

TRI pheth a ddylid i bob gwraig dda gan ei gwr: cariad ffyddlon, ymgeledd tirion, a bodd ei chalon.

TRI pheth a wnant wraig yn anniwair: wyneb têg, pen ffôl, a chalon falch.

TRI pheth a barant i wraig briod gael cas yn lle cariad: bod yn anynad, chwenych blaenori, a bod yn dda wrth ei bol ei hun.

TRI pheth a ddygant barch i wraig: ymadroddion pwyllus, boddlondeb i'r byd a fo arni, a bod yn heddychgar y'mhlith ei chymydogion.

Y pethau a ddylai fod ar bob gwraig er boddloni ei gwr ydynt fel hyn,

Yn dawel ei hyspryd, yn serchog ei hwynebpryd, a'i dwylaw yn ddiwyd.

Ei thŷ yn drefnus, yn ei gorchwyl yn fedrus, a'i phlant yn fagwriaethus.

Yn gyfiawn ei bwriad, a meddwl ananllad, a buchedd ddiafrad.

UFUDD-DOD rhywiog, genau tawedog, a gwylder serchog.

Yn hoyw yn ei thro, yn gyflym ei dwylo, a'i gorchwyl yn gryno.

Ei llafar yn rhadlon, yn hael ei chalon, ac yn gweled ei digon.

UNLLAW yn casglu, llaw arall yn rhanu, a'i phen yn pryderu.

Ei deall yn llathraidd, ei gwybodau yn deuluaidd, a'i moesau yn foneddigaidd.

Yn brydferth ei hymddwyn, yn erchi yn addfwyn, ac yn gwrando ar bob cwyn.

Ei theulu yn ei chanmol, ei deddfau yn rhinweddol, a'i phlant yn ei hysgol.

Ei saig yn flasus, ei hannerch yn weddus, a'i derbyn yn serchus.

Yn cael parch doethion, clod ei chymydogion, a bendith y tlodion.

Yn hyfforddi yn gall, yn gwilied rhag gwall, ac yn meithrin ei phlant yn famawl.

Yn amyneddus, yn dangnefeddus, ac yn rhinweddus.

Yn fonheddig ei moesau, yn roesawgar ei geiriau, ac yn Grist'nogaidd ei defodau.

Yn ddoeth ei llawenydd, yn welleugar ei cherydd, ac yn gydwybodlawn ei chrefydd.

——o——

Y wraig a fyddo fel hyn a gerir gan ei gwr a'i theulu, a chan bawb a'i hadnappo.——a gwyn ei fyd y gwr a'i meddi.

TREFRIW, ARGRAFFWYD GAN J. JONES, DROS H. HUGHES.

Trioedd y Gwragedd, by Hugh Hughes, 1821.

The iconography of both pictures and text in Hugh Hughes's *Trioedd y Gwragedd* reveals the complicated interaction of intellectual and popular opinion where they meet in the popular press. Hughes was upwardly mobile—though born into a poor farming family of Methodists he had emigrated to Liverpool and by 1821 was coming under the influence of a wide range of ideas concerning Wales and the world. His choice of triads as a textual form to speak to the class he had left behind and now wished to instruct, reflected his discovery of the antiquarian patriotism of the eighteenth century. But the triads were used to deliver a message which belongs to the Nonconformism and Utilitarianism which would dominate nineteenth-century intellectual life in Wales. The first picture presents ignorance, a domestic scene of disorder and sluttishness; the second, where reason and Christian principles are at work, presents the happy family of mother, father and child gathered together around the icon of an open book. The printed word and picture are depicted here as the source of moral and material improvement.

Both Methodism in the period of the great revival of the middle of the eighteenth century, and Chartism in the first half of the nineteenth century, were great popular movements which might be claimed to represent the

Mae rwan ryw sect newydd,
A ymglydodd dros y gwledydd;
A'r nadau hyll annedwydd,
Ynfydrwydd drwg anfedrus,
Yn twyllo bobol weiniaid air,
Tecca sysmaticiaid
Gau athrawon ddylion ddeiliaid
Pen weiniaid a phiniwnus.

Castell Dinas Bran from Llangollen, by Richard Wilson, 1770-1, detail.

voice of the people. The contemporary ballads almost exclusively condemn both movements, also in the name of the people. John Cadwalad regarded the Methodists as mad fanatics, disturbing the tranquillity of the times by deceiving the people:

And now there comes a new sect,
Spreading through the nations,
With its ugly miserable ranting,
Its evil, ugly idiocy
Deceiving the innocent people,
Fine schismatics!
False prophets, blind fools,
Bigoted nincompoops.[18]

John Cadwalad's ballad may have reflected the views of some of the ordinary people; it certainly reflected the views of the establishment and of figures like Sir Watkin Williams Wynn, much celebrated in contemporary ballads for his relentless harassing of Methodists. Frequent references in the period to Methodists as "Pengryniaid"—roundheads—indicate the length of the folk memory and the deeply ingrained loyalty of many Welsh people to the monarchy and the social order over which it presided. Methodism was perceived as Puritanism revived and was reviled as much because it threatened the established order as because of its religious content. However uncomfortable that order might be for the often hungry people, it was, in the opinion of most ballad writers, better than the disorder which they associated with the religious enthusiasm of the 1640s. To what extent the people agreed, in view of the spectacular success of Methodism, is arguable. The hymns of Pantycelyn and later Methodist writers would prove a more pervasive influence than the ballads of John Cadwalad and his like-minded contemporaries, however well they sold at the time. A century later, Methodist and other non-conformist hymns were regularly printed in the ballad sheet form, and the good old Church of England, loyally defended in the Welsh popular literature of the eighteenth century, was the object of derision.[19]

John Cadwalad presented the people as innocents, vulnerable to the deceits of anti-social radicals, a common theme in the ballads of the eighteenth and nineteenth centuries. The same image of innocence is presented in the high-art paintings of Richard Wilson done for the benefit of a patrician audience, notably the figures in the foreground of his *Castell Dinas Bran from Llangollen,* painted in 1770-1 for Sir Watkin Williams Wynn, son of the anti-Methodist. It comes as no surprise to find Ywain Meirion, still touched in the mid-nineteenth century by the faint memory of an ancient tradition of professional poets composing paeans of praise to the same patrician class, writing a poem in celebration of the third Sir Watkin, son of Wilson's patron. It seems most unlikely that either John Cadwalad or Ywain Meirion reflected a perception that the people held of themselves as vulnerable innocents. They spoke, at least in part, the

21

Ein gwlad a lanwyd o elynion,
Dadleuon croesion trymion trist,
Gan wrthryfela yn bena' beunydd,
Er attal cynnydd crefydd Crist;

Cychwyn wnaeth yn sir Drefaldwyn,
Yn y gwanwyn gyda gwg,
Ond nid oedd hyn wrth wyr y Dehau,
Mewn dychryn draw ond dechrau drwg.

Roedd eraill yn nghym'dogaeth Merthyr,
Yn eithaf prysur yr un pryd;
Yn hudo'r gweithwyr ac areithio,
Ar hyd yr ardal hono o hyd;

Ond yoedd hyn yn waith truenus,
Ac arswydus i bob sir;
I'r rhei'ny godi ar ddydd yr Arglwydd,
Yn erbyn grym cyfreithiau'r tir.

Gwell ymostwng nac ymryson,
Trwy'r deyrnas hon, rhag troion trais;
A geiriau synwyr gwyr y senedd,
All wrando'n llon bob cyson gais.

thoughts of someone else.

Typical conservatism in the face of a popular movement was displayed by Ywain Meirion in a ballad against the Chartists. The occasion was the rising in Newport in 1839, but he reminded his audience of earlier movements in Llanidloes and Merthyr, and condemned them all. The Chartist leaders were bewitching their innocent adherents among the people as the Methodist ranters had done before:

Our land is overrun with evil,
All in contention, heavy, sad,
Revolt, each day, against the good news,
The word of God, the tidings glad;

It began in fair Montgomery,
A spring of troubles, year of frowns,
Yet this was nothing to what followed,
Men of the south, by terror drowned.

Some others in the mills of Merthyr
Prepared themselves to join the fray;
Deceived the people with their speeches,
All round the town, both night and day.[20]

The thrust of many ballads towards social and political conservatism was often associated with a strong hint that since the established order of things was God's work, disturbance was blasphemous and certain to result in punishment in hell which would be very disagreable. Ywain Meirion complained not only that the Chartists had rioted but that they had done so on a Sunday:

This was, indeed, a frightful business,
Spreading fear throughout the land;
That they should rise up on the Sabbath
'Gainst the law to make their stand.

The message to the people was leave it to your betters to decide what is right and proper for you:

'Tis better to submit than argue,
For fear that hate this kingdom taint;
In parliament men speak with wisdom,
And hear in peace each just complaint.

It is clear, therefore, that the ballad and the popular visual image, far from being simply a mirror of the mind of a homogenous populace, were active forces in a complicated cultural debate.

Nevertheless, beyond conflicting opinion on matters of the day, the emerging popular press did have a homogenising effect of profound significance for Wales, in two ways. From the time of Thomas Jones's almanacks, the popular press addressed the whole Welsh nation and only the Welsh nation. In so doing, it encouraged a sense both of internal coherence and of distinctness through the language itself and its content when this was also Welsh. However, paradoxically, the popular press was also a vital medium for the development of fundamental assumptions of British rather than Welsh identity in the people. Like cinema and television in the twentieth century, it was a great enemy of the fragile relationship between a particular tradition and a particular place, even through the difference of language between Wales and England. This effect was not a kind of averaging out between forces of equal strength, but the invasion of one set of perceptions by another. The traffic in translations was one-way, bringing in legends such as Robin Hood and Dick Turpin, and putting English versions of archetypes such as Sir John Barleycorn into Welsh costume as Syr John Heidden, or Siôn Haidd. A murder in Islington, picked up from an English newspaper or ballad, was as often recorded in a Welsh ballad, accompanied by a picture of the scene at Tyburn, as a murder in Cardigan, subtly reinforcing a British framework for life.

For most ordinary people in the countryside—who never saw England or an English person—the British framework must have had little practical relevance but nevertheless became the unit from which they perceived the wider world. Most obviously in its description of London politics, of the foreign and imperial business of the state, and the ceremonial of state institutions, the popular press was the agent of British consciousness. Ywain Meirion's appeal to his listeners to leave decision-taking to their betters in London encouraged a well established cult of parliament, which, along with the monarchy (even when lampooned) and tokens of the people such as John Bull, all had a strong homogenising tendency by providing an iconography of shared symbols.

In the same year as his *Trioedd y Gwragedd*, Hugh Hughes also had John Jones print a closely integrated text and pictures of *The Landing of His Majesty, George the Fourth, at Holyhead*, which exemplifies the power of the word and the visual image in the propagation of symbols of the Union.

The Execution of Dick Turpin, by an unknown engraver, from *Bywyd Turpin Leidr,* published by John Jones, Llanrwst, 1835.

23

The Landing of His Majesty, George the Fourth, at Holyhead, August 7th, 1821, by Hugh Hughes, 1821.

The King, on his way to Ireland, had been prevailed upon to come ashore at Holyhead, the first English monarch to set foot in Wales for centuries. Hughes's large wood engraving was the most ambitious he ever made, and stretched the technology available to John Jones to the limit. The black line borders had to be done separately and the picture stuck on. It cost him £2·15·0d. The sheet also carried a small keyed block to identify the participants named in the sycophantic description of the "indescribable joy" felt by the inhabitants of Anglesey at the king's condescension:

"His Majesty was assisted to land from his barge by two Gentlemen, who handed ropes to him, and he ascended the steps without difficulty, and landed on the shores of Cambria, greeted by the most enthusiastic cheers. His Majesty remained some time on the Pier and bowed most graciously to the enraptured assembly. The Royal Marine Band stood near the spot, playing God save the King."

The great irony of this production, as we shall see, is that the loyal Welsh perception of the English king was in marked contrast to the cynicism displayed by the English popular press in recording the same event.

Comparison of the treatment of the Welsh in the English popular press and the perceptions of Welsh people themselves reveal many such ironies. The English popular press, as agent of British homogeneity, in so far as it concerned itself directly with Wales at all did so largely by projecting a stereotype of the nation that was seldom endearing and—especially before about 1740 (when the Scots came along to bear the xenophobic brunt)—was often virulent in its abuse. This material seems to have engendered little sense of outrage, certainly not sufficient to stimulate a political backlash, but rather a resigned and self-pitying acceptance of the injustice of it all and a continued stress on Welsh loyalty with exhortations to the people to do even better in future.

The remarkable addiction of the Welsh to the idea of the British family, so obvious in the popular press, was certainly sustained by the common bond of Protestant religion in a Catholic Europe, but it can only be ultimately explained by the much older idea that Britishness was a Welsh invention—that modern Britain was a return to an ancient *status quo* when the Welsh had indeed been the Britons, inhabitants of the whole island.[21]

BRAD Y CYLLILL HIRION.....GWEL DAL. 102.

Drwy frâd y Cyllill hirion,
Mawr sôn drwy Gymru sydd,
Fe gwympai'n mawrion bendefigion,
Rai dewrion yn eu dydd...

An important agent for the persistence of this world-view was Theophilus Evans's hugely popular account of Welsh history, *Drych y Prif Oesoedd*, first published by Siôn Rhydderch at Shrewsbury in 1716. Its focal point was the coming to the islands of Britain of the English, and their betrayal of their British (that is, Welsh) hosts at Stonehenge on the Night of the Long Knives. The account was frequently recycled in ballads and in the work of the *beirdd gwlad* or popular poets such as William Edward, Eos Padarn, writing in 1826:

Brad y Cyllill Hirion, by Hugh Hughes, published by John Jones, Llanrwst in *Drych y Prif Oesoedd*, 1822.

> The treachery of the long knives,
> Through Wales is told with rage,
> Our leaders, bold, who lost their lives,
> The bravest of the age...[22]

When John Jones of Llanrwst reprinted *Drych y Prif Oesoedd* for the umpteenth time in 1822, he included—for the first time—an illustration. Significantly, the chosen scene was the Night of the Long Knives, *Brad y Cyllill Hirion*, depicted by Hugh Hughes. Gwrtheyrn, the only Welsh leader to escape with his life, attacks the English with an iron bar he has found lying nearby. In the 1820s there was considerable interest in the veracity of this story. It had been repeated in John Hughes's celebrated history *Horae Britannicae*, in 1819, which was probably the source of Hugh Hughes's image, and also in 1822, the Gwent Eisteddfod offered a prize for an essay on the subject.[23]

However, despite this treachery, the ultimate message of Welsh history as expounded in *Drych y Prif Oesoedd* was that after centuries of disturbance, providence had eventually put things back into their intended condition by the reunification of Britain under the Welsh King Henry VII. Britain was a Welsh idea that the English, reluctantly, had had to accept with the Tudor monarchy. Eos Padarn's version of the story, in erratic doggerel shot through with middle-class tradesman's values, goes something like this:

> When Harry Tudor took the throne
> 'Twas done to make us free
> Of our oppressors, full of spite,
> So brothers we could be...

25

Coroni Harri'r Seithfed
A wnaed, i'n gwared ni
O'n gorthrymder, rhai llawn digter
Wnai'n froder o un fri;
Nyni hyd yn bresenol yn frodyr siriol sydd,
Mae'r holl Saeson a'r Cymry'n ddigon
Heddychlon er ei ddydd...

Yn lle rhyfela'n greulon,
Yn sylwlon, er lleshad,
Mae'r Saeson mwyn-gu'n cyd fasnachu
A'r Cymry'n ddi nacâd;
Clawdd Offa sy'n ddi effaith,
Ac eilwaith ni fydd, gwn,
I Sais na Chymro'i adgyweirio,
Cair teithio heibion i hwn,
A throsto rhodio'n rhydd
A gawn, nid bod tan gudd,
Yn holltau'r creigiau fel bu'n cyndadau,
Diau, er's llawer dydd...

Evan Lloyd, G. Marchi
after J. Berridge, c.1772,
detail.

Instead of cruel fighting
The good of all to do
The gentle English trade in Wales
Our business we pursue.
Old *Offa's Dyke* is fallen
And there will be no need
For them or us to close the gap
We travel through at speed.
Through the breach we freely steer
And may be seen, full clear,
Unlike our forebears, years ago
Who hid themselves for fear...

Wales had bestowed three blessings on the English, which by the mid-eighteenth century had become fundamental to their British idea. The problem was that the English continually failed to appreciate the nationality of their benefactors and had a persistent tendency to revert to type. The first blessing was Christianity itself, preserved and fought for in Wales when the pagan Saxons had turned traitor and driven the Welsh westwards. This self-perception of the almost innate Christianity of the Welsh was reinforced repeatedly as the English strayed from the essential Protestant Britishness which their state church was supposed to define. The Anglican Church had decayed to such an extent in Wales in the eighteenth century, that the great Methodist Revival had been required to set things straight. Again, in the mid-nineteenth century, Puseyism, frequently attacked in the Welsh popular press, demonstrated the regressive tendencies of the English. The second blessing, associated in particular with Henry VII, was an orderly state, a situation which the English had disturbed in the Civil War of the 1640s. The third was nothing less than the idea of freedom itself. Wales was the home of freedom since it had been the Welsh who had fought for the independence of the islands against a succession of invaders—Romans, Saxons and Normans.

The belief that Great Britain was a Welsh idea and that its blessings of Christianity, stability and freedom were Welsh blessings was explicitly raised time and again in the popular press and lies hidden behind attitudes to other issues on which it passed comment.

The association of freedom with Welshness was a perception particularly beloved of the gentry and of intellectuals. It was maintained in the face of a long history of satirical comment on what the English regarded as an absurd conceit and was usually set unflatteringly side by side with depictions of the poverty-stricken contemporary condition of the people. Nevertheless, in the second half of the eighteenth century, the idea achieved some credibility among the English intellectual community who acceded to a vague concept of the Welsh as aboriginal Britons. It coincided with the high point of English political and social satire in writing and in the prints. As a consequence, to be Welsh and well connected in London in the 1760s and 70s could be exhilarating. It is clear from the correspondence of high-profile people such as the satirist Evan Lloyd, that Welsh intellectuals both sought each other's company and moved easily in the world of English radicals and *bons viveurs* in London amongst whom the idea of Welshness as a kind of living archaeology of Englishness took hold.

This was also the period of the Welsh tour—of the examination of the face of the country itself, as well as of the faces of its representatives in London. In Wales, an ancient people occupied a mountain landscape in a visible if faint reflection of the Rousseau-esque natural condition of man. Or so the image was constructed in the eighteenth-century game of ideas, a fantasy which writers such as Lloyd, and painters such as Wilson, encouraged in their own interests. Evan Lloyd was a friend of John Wilkes. In 1771 he wrote to the the prophet of liberty from his home near Bala:

"If Milton was right when he called Liberty a mountain nymph, I am now writing to you from her residence; and the peaks of our Welch Alps heighten the idea by wearing the clouds of Heaven like a cap of Liberty".[24]

The image of the Last Bard, who had killed himself among those Alps rather than submit to the tyranny of the English King Edward I, came to exemplify this idea. However, until well into the nineteenth century and the popularisation of the Eisteddfod movement, the Bard remained a stubbornly high-art image.[25] Despite the closeness of Evan Lloyd and his circle to the core of fashion, the Welsh as Ancient Britons were lampooned in the popular prints, though not, it is true, with the earlier ferocity. These prints were very much a London phenomenon, the object of little published comment and probably having minimal effect on popular consciousness in Wales itself. Religion and its images were a different matter, both as an expression of national self-perception and in the effect that peculiarly Welsh attitudes had on the development of words and pictures in the popular press.

The most common subject matter of the popular press all over Europe was, from the beginning, religion. In Wales, religious images, like other *genres*, defined homogeneity of two different and conflicting kinds. The British were, as a whole, Protestant and saw themselves in opposition to the Catholicism common to the enemies of the state. The most popular books (though these were not always the same as popular literature since many remained expensive) were, in Wales as in England, Bunyan's *Pilgrim's Progress* and Foxe's *Book of Martyrs*. The most ambitious product of the Welsh press in the early nineteenth century was Thomas Jones of Denbigh's *Hanes Diwygwyr, Merthyron a Chyffeswyr Eglwys Lloegr* (The History of the Reformers, Martyrs, and Confessors of the Church of England), copiously illustrated with woodcuts. Ironically, however, Thomas Jones's massive adaptation of Foxe emerged from the press of Thomas Gee only two years after the Welsh Methodists had left the Church of England amid accusations of sedition and disloyalty, in 1811. Protestantism was certainly the philosophical core around which British consciousness coagulated, but contrarily, differences within Protestantism provided one of the main sources of a re-emergent Welsh sense of distinctness. Especially after its Welsh dimension, largely congruent with the language, was brought into clear focus by Methodist dissent, Nonconformism became not only a definitive characteristic of Welsh nationhood, but also, in the minds of many, definitive of Welsh superiority over the English. Occupation of the religious high ground became a substitute for marginal political status. A characteristic expression of this view was the Reverend David Davies' popular book of stories *Echoes from the Welsh Hills*, illustrated by T.H.Thomas in 1883:

"It is the Protestant Christianity of the Welsh people, as lived and taught by their religious teachers during the last two centuries and a half, that has

preserved them from ignorance, lawlessness, and irreligion, and made of them one of the most scripturally-enlightened, loyal and religious nations on the face of the earth."

One of the most important characteristics of the popular visual culture of Wales in the nineteenth century was its use of the images of Nonconformist religious leaders. Emanating mainly from originals produced by artisan painters, engravings of ministers became icons of the nation. They were not, however, usually coupled with texts except by implication, since the most popular images of all were those of the great preachers, especially John Elias and Christmas Evans. Only in the posthumous memoir, which developed strict conventions of literary form and often included a portrait as the frontispiece, did picture and text come physically together. Given, on the one hand, the frequent use of hymns in the ballad sheet form and, on the other, the cult of the preacher (who was often also the hymn writer), it is surprising that hymns were not printed with woodcut versions of the intaglio engravings of their authors. Only a very few portraits of national figures were reproduced as wood engravings, and there is only one religious amongst them, the Reverend David Peter of Carmarthen, done by Hugh Hughes.

The memoirs sometimes recounted the taking of a minister's portrait. A description of his display of reluctance to acquiesce in this sin of pride and his eventual agreement, under pressure from his colleagues who say that familiarity with the features of such a paragon of virtue will encourage morality in the people, became a common motif.[26] Religious leaders at a national and at a local level liked to emphasise their awareness of the Puritan tradition of their faith and its rejection of images, in contrast to the Catholic's idolatry. The painter Samuel Maurice Jones remembered one "old saint", a deacon of his chapel, being "extremely troublesome on hearing that I was beginning to study the arts. He felt strongly that the church authorities should turn their attention to the matter, and that those responsible for doctrine should look into the case. Did not the scripture say, and that in the Ten Commandments—the law of moral and eternal life and salvation—'Thou shalt not make unto thee any graven image'."[27]

For people of this persuasion, the word was the source of knowledge and it stood in contrast to the image. The Protestant Reformation, reacting against the mystique which had put an elite priesthood between God and the illiterate people, had available to it the new technology of printing and

Cofiaf yn dda i un o'r cyfryw fynd yn hynod o boenus wrth ddeall fy mod i yn dechreu efrydu'r Celfau. Teimlai yn gryf y dylai'r awdurdodau yn yr eglwys roddi sylw i'r mater ac i'r rhai a ofalent am yr athrawiaeth edrych i mewn i'r achos! Oni ddywedai'r ysgrythur, a hynny yn y Deng Air Deddf,—rheol foesol a thragwyddol bywyd ac ymarweddiad—oni ddywedai hi yn bendant, 'Na wna *lun* dim?'

Yr Argraphwâsg (medd y doethion) yw Canwyll y Byd a Rhyddid PLANT PRYDAIN.... Pam i ninnau (a fûom wŷr Glewion gynt! os oes coel arnom) na cheisiwn bêth o'r Goleuni?

Tri dyben sydd mewn golwg yn rhoddiad y darluniadau yn yr Addysgydd. 1. Difyrwch i bob un. 2. Cynnorthwy i rai ddyall ac ystyried y peth a ddarlunir, a'i amgylchiadau. 3. Cael achlysur i son am bethau hynod a grybwyllir yn yr ysgrythyrau.

---

so was able to liberate the word—which had the effect of emphasising it anew. In contrast to the dangerous distraction of the visual image it was perceived as unambiguous and definitive. It was the word of God, not the image of God, which carried the meaning of God.

In nineteenth-century Wales, by association of ideas, not only the word of God but almost any word, if printed, attracted a reverential attitude as the means to both salvation and material progress for individual and nation alike. In 1735, proposing the establishment of a press at Llannerchymedd by public subscription, Lewis Morris had predicted the received opinion of the next century:

"The printing press (*say the wise*) is the Light of the World and the Freedom of the CHILDREN OF BRITAIN... Why should we (who were once Brave men! if we believe in ourselves) not reach for our share of enlightenment?"[28]

The visual image became itself a great promoter of the virtues of the word. Scenes of adults and children reading often adorned printed ballads and cheap books. For Hugh Hughes, as we have seen, the word was a particularly resonant motif. His depiction of a respectable bourgeois gentleman reading an improving tract in his study, engraved for *Allwedd Duwinyddiaeth* (The Key to Theology) in 1823, reflected his own experience as an upwardly mobile, Methodist auto-didact.

Nevertheless, as late as 1858, Samuel Roberts of Llanbrynmair remarked that although the arts of painting and literature were similar to each other, "literature is the more useful",[29] reflecting the persistent view that the two were at best in a hierarchical relationship, if not, in fact, opposed. In 1821, even Hughes (who had painted Samuel Roberts's father) had felt the need to justify the inclusion of pictures in texts in *Yr Addysgydd*. He did so partly in terms of their ability to elucidate the fundamental word. He wrote:

"We have three objectives in view by including pictures in *Yr Addysgydd*, 1. Entertainment for all. 2. To aid the understanding of the event portrayed, and its circumstances. 3. To have occasion to talk of the extraordinary things contained in the scriptures."[30]

However, Hugh Hughes's remarks are misleading evidence if we wish to go beyond the image of Wales constructed by pious Nonconformist

Robert Jones, Rhoslan, lithograph by B.Finney after Hugh Hughes, published by John Jones, Llanrwst, in Cofiant... Mr Robert Jones, Dinas, 1834.

29

Y Parch. D. Peter, Athraw Duwinyddol Athrofa Caerfyrddin, by Hugh Hughes, published in *Y Dysgedydd Crefyddol* 1823.

Reading, by Hugh Hughes, published by John Evans in *Allwedd Duwinyddiaeth*, 1823.

patriots and try to understand the perceptions of the majority. Hughes offered his apologia because he knew that amongst critical observers of his publication would be prominent religious leaders of the same persuasion as Samuel Roberts who clung to the residual prejudice against images. Hughes was certainly not apologising to the bulk of his audience. In 1827, the editors of *Yr Athraw i Blentyn* (The Child's Teacher), another Sunday School magazine for which he engraved, were more forthright:

"Since next year's issues of *Yr Athraw* are to be decorated with pictures, the profit to go to the work of propagating the Gospel, we anticipate your continued support."[31]

From the age of fourteen, Hughes had spent much of his time in printing offices where he not only observed closely the workings of the popular press but came to admire its power. As we shall see, from the 1830s to the 1860s Welsh publishers produced cheap religious imagery in substantial quantities, coinciding with the rise to its establishment pinnacle of Nonconformism. This wealth of visual evidence of the attitudes of the people has been ignored by historians working in the pious Puritan intellectual tradition. The material confirms the great appetite in the people for pictures that Hughes, John Jones, James Cope and others had recognised, and demonstrates that it had little to do with the elucidation of texts. Most of the population were literate. The people liked pictures and liked them for themselves.

" A ſhan ei gymmeryd ef erbyn ei ddeheulaw
efe a'i cyfododd ef i fynu, ac yn ebrwydd ei draed
ef a'i fferau a gadarnhawyd."

NID llawer, mae'n debyg, o'r rhai a
allant ddarllen yr Addysgydd, i'w
ddeall, sydd heb allu cofio yn union wrth
ddarllen yr adnod uchod, Yn 1. Pwy
oedd *Efe* a gymmerodd erbyn ei law
ddyn cloff o groth ei fam, ac annalluog i
symud, fel y codai, y safai, y rhodiai, ac
y neidiai. Yn 2. Yn enw pwy, trwy
nerth neu awdurdod pwy (ei hunan, ynte
rhyw un arall) y gwnaeth yr *Efe* yma y
weithred ryfeddol.

Y CAMEL.

" Ti (Arglwydd) a greaist bob peth; ac o herwydd dy ewyllys di y maent, ac y crewyd
hwynt.—Dat. 4, 11.

Y CAWRFIL, o'r hwn y mae y darlun uchod, a ddangoswyd ychydig
wythnosau yn ol yn Nghaerfyrddin.—Y
cyfryw o ddarllenwyr yr Addysgydd ar
nas cawsant o'r blaen gyfleusdra i wybod
peth o hanes, a golygiad anifail sy mor
enwog yn yr Ysgrythyrau, mae'n debyg, a
fyddant hoff o weled yr hyn a osodir yma
ger eu bronau.

ℂ The fyrst boke of the

Introduction of Knowledge. The whych dothe teache a man to speake parte of all maner of languages, and to know the vsage and fashion of all maner of countreys. And for to know the moste parte of all maner of coynes of money, the whych is currant in euery region. Made by Andrew Borde, of Physycke Doctor. Dedycated to the right honorable & gracious lady Mary daughter of our Souerayne Lorde Kyng Henry the eyght.

32

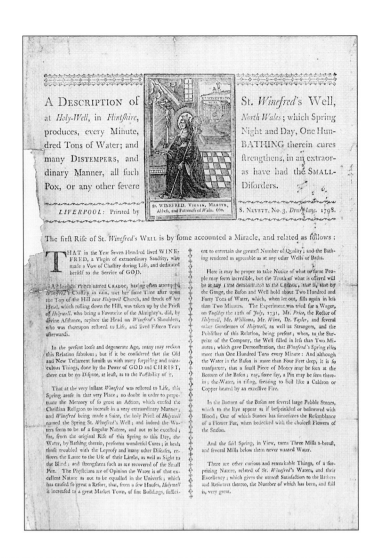

A Description of St. Winnefred's Well, printed by S. Nevett, Liverpool, 1798.

Enjoys the Habitation—Hence, the prompt
Concern to chear Distress when the rude Waves
Drive the tall Vessel bulging on the Rocks
Ingulph'd: the miserable Crew, apall'd,
And resembling, from the Wreck escap'd,
Find hospitable Aid—True, the fierce Stares
Of Passion, wearing in our Souls deform
The Frame, of Nature; Does not this become
The candid, open, undesigning Man?
Yes, avaricious Custom first impos'd
A Curb on Reason—who despite the Chain!
Scorn the deep, formal *Syren* Smile of sly
Hypocrisy; the vile, invidious Phrase
Of smooth Betrayers; with a *Spartan* Grace
Speak the blunt Dictates of the Soul;... But when
The big Emotion of exulting Thought
Subsides, the rough *Isnian* lull'd to Rest,
Knows not a stiller Calm the Heav'nly Sphere
Round the bright Sun no more harmonious Rol
Eternal Order, than each tuneful Pulse
With equal Measure fluctuates the Heart.

The author of these lines is unknown but they are similar in tone to the work of John Dyer who celebrated the landscape of Wales in *Grongar Hill*, published in 1726. Dyer's *The Fleece*, begun in 1743, was published in 1757, precisely the period of the print.

In the companion piece, the premature demise of Shon-ap-Morgan brings Unnafred to the metropolis. Her husband has "died of a surfeit, having grown extravagant in London, and made a great meal of leeks and sheese and red-herrings, on St David's-day, among his countrymen, at

50

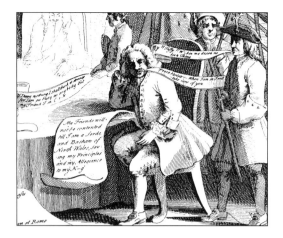

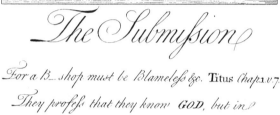

belief that "The *English* were never able to conquer the *Welch*; who were artfully seduced in their allegiance to Edward II, of England...." The second edition of *Drych y Prif Oesoedd*, which nurtured this perception among Welsh speakers, had recently been published. It might be that Theophilus Evans was the author of the text on the print, although he did not live among the London Welsh. It certainly follows his historical analysis closely in its subsequent reference to the blessings of the Tudor succession. Sir Watkin Williams Wynn, at this period beginning to attract the attention of the English satirists producing intaglio prints, rates a mention, since he "thought it an Honour to be called a Welchman". The whole defence is concluded by some distinctly high-brow verse for a popular print, describing the virtues of the country and the people with only a passing reference to the passionate stereotype:

> The wholesome Air diffuses on our Cheeks
> The Rosy Blush of Health or on the Brow
> Enthron'd with Modesty, the little Hue
> Of Beauty reigns, as in the Vernal Morn.
> Rich in our Bosoms spring the tender seeds
> Of kind HUMANITY there, at their Home.
> Sincerity and faithful Friendship meet;
> The plain good Heart, accompany'd with Truth

Poor Taff, by an unknown engraver, c. 1780.

Shon-ap-Morgan, Shentleman of Wales... published by William Dicey, London, c. 1747.

Unnafred Shones, wife to Shon-ap-Morgan... published by William Dicey, London, c. 1747.

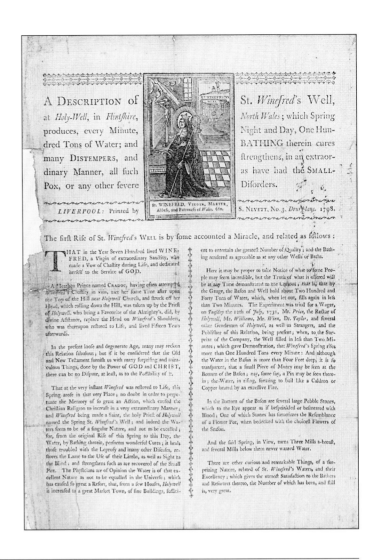

Enjoys the Habitation—Hence, the prompt
Concern to chear Distress when the rude Waves
Drive the tall Vessel bulging on the Rocks
Ingulph'd: the miserable Crew, apall'd,
And resembling, from the Wreck escap'd,
Find hospitable Aid—True, the fierce Stares
Of Passion, wearing in our Souls deform
The Frame, of Nature; Does not this become
The candid, open, undesigning Man?
Yes, avaricious Custom first impos'd
A Curb on Reason—who despite the Chain!
Scorn the deep, formal *Syren* Smile of sly
Hypocrisy; the vile, invidious Phrase
Of smooth Betrayers; with a *Spartan* Grace
Speak the blunt Dictates of the Soul;... But when
The big Emotion of exulting Thought
Subsides, the rough *Isnian* lull'd to Rest,
Knows not a stiller Calm the Heav'nly Sphere
Round the bright Sun no more harmonious Rol
Eternal Order, than each tuneful Pulse
With equal Measure fluctuates the Heart.

The author of these lines is unknown but they are similar in tone to the
work of John Dyer who celebrated the landscape of Wales in *Grongar Hill,*
published in 1726. Dyer's *The Fleece*, begun in 1743, was published in
1757, precisely the period of the print.

In the companion piece, the premature demise of Shon-ap-Morgan brings
Unnafred to the metropolis. Her husband has "died of a surfeit, having
grown extravagant in London, and made a great meal of leeks and
sheese and red-herrings, on St David's-day, among his countrymen, at

their great annual feast, and drank plentifully of strong drinks he had never tasted before." The use of Winifred as a characteristic Welsh name reflects the familiarity of Saint Winifred to the English audience from an early date. St Winifred's well at Holywell was one of the few Welsh places known in England, much visited on pilgrimage and for healing. Even in the mid-eighteenth century, when the fashion for picturesque Welsh tours was just beginning, it was generating advertising material. *A Description of St. Winefred's Well...*, printed in Liverpool by John Saddler in 1753, was illustrated with a fine woodcut of the building and of the martyrdom. By 1798, a very similar sheet with a good copy of the original block was produced in Liverpool by Nevett (perhaps the master of Hugh Hughes), and a third version, with a more naive rendering of the scene soon followed, printed in Holywell itself. Sometime after 1829 a fourth version was produced locally with a block which omitted the martyrdom, perhaps reflecting a desire to keep the image of the place in tune with the more squeamish sensitivities of the period.

The text of *UNNAFRED SHONES, wife to Shon-ap-Morgan*, was certainly written by a different author to that which complements her husband's print—it is a conventional Wenglish satire of the milder kind. "An INVENTORY of the Goods of UNNAFRED SHONES, made for fear she should not return", includes such items as "One Toasting-fork, which my poor Shonny toasted his sheese with for many a goot year, cot pless his memory," and:

"Two mouse-traps, besure set them, for feer the mice should eat the sheese and then I shall have nothing to eat when I return. One piece of bacon, but I shall take that in my pocket, for fear there should be no bacon in London. Six milch goats. Two kids. One cat, pray take care of poor Tabby, and give her Milk when you milk the goats. One bed of leeks growing, besides a bushel in the house. And Forty one red-herrings."

The funeral sermon clearly sold well for the print makers. The same image of Shon-ap-Morgan is repeated in reverse in a much smaller woodcut above a very similar text, printed, we are told, in Glangothan itself for "Shon-ap-Morgan,-ap-Rice, at the Sheshire-Sheese, in Leak Sreet". He was accompanied on his journey to London by a block based on the common original repeated on the Newcastle Sheffrey Morgan, but much finer, with his inverted sword making a good suggestive joke.

A Historical Description of St. Winefred's Well, printed by James Davies, Holywell, c. 1829.

51

III Personal satires—the Welsh in London

By the mid-eighteenth century the intaglio processes of line engraving and etching on copper were emerging as a medium for original work in England, rather than simply as a means of reproducing painted images. They soon became the dominant medium for visual satire, since they allowed for more subtle characterisation than woodcuts in the age in which personal caricature of individuals emerged, as distinct from stereotyping. The woodcut became confined, for a period, to the very bottom of the market—to the illustration of ballads, advertisements and posters. The new cartoons were certainly derivatives of the ballads, broadsides and chapbooks which had given the public a taste for political comment. Nevertheless, they took on a life of their own, broadening the market and taking it off the streets and into specialist print shops. The new prints responded immediately to the political issues and social scandals of the day, but were more expensive than a ballad or broadside. Specialist shops such as Bowles' Map and Print Warehouse in St Paul's Churchyard, and Mat Darley's Macaroni Print Shop in the Strand, flourished. These prints, so strongly rooted in London life, certainly found their way into booksellers shops in the towns on the borders of Wales, but to what extent they were sold in the towns of Wales itself is difficult to ascertain. In London, their appeal would have been broadly based, but in Wales, the audience sufficiently familiar with the social and political context of the cartoons to understand their meaning must have been confined to those among the gentry and the intelligentsia who read the English newspapers. One Welsh intellectual, Thomas Johnes of Hafod, took a particular interest in them. In his bravura manner, he ordered a copy of every caricature ever published.

The work of William Hogarth had an important influence on the emergence of the genre. His great series, including *The Rake's Progress*, were rooted in the popular moralities of the interlude and the ballads and broadsides but were copied after original paintings and influenced by Dutch engraving. Hogarth interested himself in the day to day foibles and politics of the city around him, developing a genre in which the balance between picture and text was reversed as compared to the woodcut tradition. It would flourish in England in the hands of a series of brilliant visual satirists, notably Thomas Rowlandson, James Gillray and George Cruikshank, into the early nineteenth century.

Hogarth himself seems only once to have made reference to the Welsh, and that in a very peripheral way. In *The Rake's Progress*, the arrest of the Rake clearly occurs on March 1st, since two of the characters depicted in the scene wear the leek. Apart from a patch on the breeches of the otherwise well dressed gentleman who observes the arrest, clearly a reference to Poor Taff, Hogarth is non-committal. However, his interpreter, John Ireland, did not let pass the opportunity for a dig, hardly warranted by the original of which he spoke. In 1791 he observed in the scene a "highborn, haughty, Welshman, with an enormous leek, and a countenance keen and lofty as his native mountains...."[1]

Following the demise of Archbishop John Williams, no Welsh person or event made sufficient impact in London to draw the attention of the print makers for nearly a century—an extraordinary dark age in Welsh life as perceived from England. It was the age of the virulent abuse of the *Wallography* of 1682 and Torbuck's disagreeable publications of 1738. However, in the decade following Torbuck's diatribe, Sir Watkin Williams Wynn, the third baronet and the first of a line of that name, began to attract the attention of the English public. Sir Watkin had made himself immensely rich by marriage and interested himself in politics. He was Member of Parliament for Denbighshire from 1716 and became a prominent Tory spokesman. The event which established the family's place in the popular prints—a place maintained through three generations, and which resulted in their becoming synonymous in the English mind with the Welsh gentry itself—was the election in 1741 for the Denbighshire seat. Sir Watkin's place was contested by his neighbours, the Myddleton family of Chirk Castle.

The Myddletons had succeeded in having one of their number made High Sheriff and therefore returning officer. William Myddleton entered false returns in favour of John Myddleton and announced him duly elected. Sir Watkin

Very Slippy Weather—Scene outside the shop of Hannah Humphrey, the printseller, in London, by Gillray, 1808.

The Arrest of the Rake, by William Hogarth, 1735.

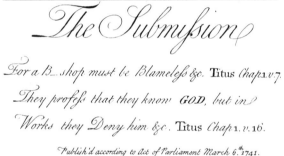

The Submission, by an unknown engraver, 1741.

The Claims of the Broad Bottom, by an unknown engraver, 1743. detail.

Reformation begun in Denbighshire, by an unknown engraver, 1741.

petitioned against the result which was overturned and the High Sheriff found himself in the unusual surroundings of the Newgate prison for seven weeks. His activities were described at the time as "The most scandalous barefaced partiality that ever was seen in a returning officer at any election".[2] *Reformation begun in Denbighshire* has him reflecting glumly on the similar circumstances of the folk hero Dick Turpin who hangs, in miniature, from a gibbet above the fireplace. A bishop contemplates his fate from beyond a barred window. This is an allusion to a third character implicated in the fraud, Bishop Maddox of Saint Asaph, who had injudiciously taken the Myddleton side during the election. The consequent embarrassment of this clergyman provided entertainment for a public informed by two versions of another print called *The Submission*. Maddox goes on bended knee before Sir Watkin to repent of his indiscretion: "Thus lowly bending I your pardon crave/Oh pity, Sir, your most obsequious slave/Who promises convicted of his crime/He'll ne'er do so again—till the next time," he whines, presumably the last phrase under his breath. An allegorical painting of the Golden Calf on the wall suggests that the Bishop has been well rewarded by the Myddletons for his campaigning on their behalf. Contested elections were an expensive business—Sir Watkin's costs in 1741 were reckoned to be £20,000. The second version of the print is more directly moralising in tone, presenting appropriate Biblical texts for the Bishop's consideration in view of his less than scrupulous behaviour.

The identification of individuals by the caricature of their features was not yet commonplace in the prints, so the faces of Sir Watkin and the Bishop are rather generalised. Indeed, in *The Submission*, Sir Watkin seems to have been borrowed from a figure in *The Rake's Progress*. In 1743, he appeared again, not dissimilar, in *The Claims of the Broad Bottom*. Sir Watkin's politics were distinctly risky in the period. He was closely associated with the Jacobite Circle of the White Rose, at one meeting of

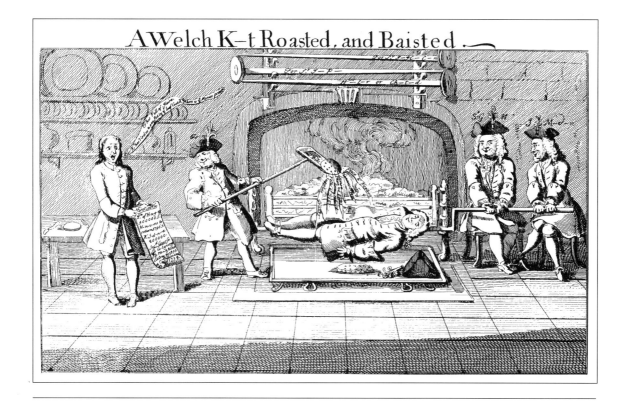

A Welch K-t Roasted, and Baisted

which he was widely believed to have burned a picture of the Hanoverian King. The petition against the Denbigh election had resulted in the first government defeat of the parliament and precipitated Walpole's fall in 1742. *The Claims of the Broad Bottom* is an unusual print in that it supports the ousted government. Various opposition figures who had demanded a coalition government (hence "broad bottom", that is, broadly based) were satirised as place-seekers and Jacobites. Sir Watkin is supported by a band of Welsh ruffians wearing leeks and carrying staves. He remarks that "My Friends will not be contented until I am a Lorde and Bashaw[3] of North Wales, saving my Principles and my Allegiance to my K..g." His supporters seem to have a rather different agenda: "By St. Taffy, Sr. W—kin we desire no such thing," they say, behind his back.

Sir Watkin's displaced opponent in 1741 had some revenge in the popular prints following the publication of a pamphlet, *An Expostulatory Epistle to the Welch Knight; or the late Revolution in Politicks; & the Extraordinary Conduct of himself and his Associates*. A print was published showing Sir Watkin turned on a spit in front of a roaring fire, entitled *A Welch K.t Roasted, and Baisted*—that is, attacked in the pamphlet. Turning the spit are a very smug John Middleton and another old enemy, Sir George Wynne of Leeswood, Flint.

The election incident is also touched upon in contemporary Welsh-language ballads, beginning to emerge in significant numbers in printed form in this period. Their concerns were significantly different to those of the London cartoons. They concentrated on Sir Watkin's hostility to Methodism, emphasising the impact that the Great Revival was having on popular consciousness in the period. Nevertheless, Ned Lloyd seems to link Sir Watkin's anti-Methodist stance with his politics. The Myddletons were in league with the "Crynion bene baw"—the dirty Roundheads. The title, translated from the eccentric Welsh, is *A ballad about the election, the wrong suffered by Sir Watkin at the hands of the roundheads...*:

> Now listen Welshmen, fit and free,
> Fair play in Wales we do not see,
> Where money, bribes and theft do work,
> This was the treachery of Chirk
> For all their fiddling and deceit,
> Sir Watkin's in, a mighty feat,
> And all the gentry on his side...

Unfortunately, none of the comment on the election from inside the culture

A Welch K-t Roasted, and Baisted, by an unknown engraver, 1745.

THE BATTLE OF BANGOR.

Gan hynu yr cymru heini hael,
Ni dous dim chwarae teg i'w gael
Mwnu ar llwunog mewn rhiw dwyn,
Yn ceisi gwnyud am frad yr Wun:
Er maint iw cwcri ai cecri ai las,
Mae Williams Wynn mewn grwym a gras
Ar holl fonedd yn i blaid...

The Battle of Bangor,
probably published by
Holland, 1796.

was complemented by specially made visual images.

Elections were the only political events that brought Wales to the attention of the English public. Over fifty years after the Bishop of St Asaph's ill-fated meddling in electoral politics, the Bishop of Bangor found himself similarly embarrassed and consequently lampooned in the London prints. It appears that the Bishop, John Warren, had been rebuffed in an attempt to get the vote and interest of his Deputy Registrar, Samuel Grindley. In revenge, he tried to relieve Grindley of his position. In his absence, the Bishop broke into his office by the cathedral and changed the locks, in the classic manner. The returning Deputy Registrar, mightily offended, broke the locks and occupied the office with a crowd of his supporters. Wielding a pistol, he defended it stoutly against a determined counter attack by the Bishop, his chaplain, two other clergymen and a lay supporter. Following the affray, Grindley went to law against the Bishop and his supporters, but the clergymen were all acquitted at Shrewsbury.

These undignified proceedings were a source of great delight to the London humorists. In *The Battle of Bangor*, published in May, 1796, some four months after the events depicted, several of the participants were named in a lampoon which stressed the Welsh context of the affair. Pitchforks are used to hurl missiles of toasted cheese and Mr Grindley wields "Owen Tudor's Pocket Pistol". The Bishop waves his crook menacingly, supported verbally by one of his curates who magnanimously shouts "Kill me and spare his Lordship" from a safe place in the shadow of his master's obese body. After the trial, in August, 1796,

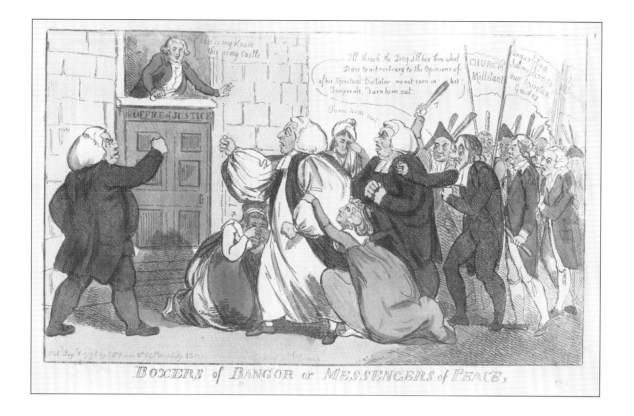

Within the image (speech bubbles and banners): "This is my House this is my Castle", "OFFICE of JUSTICE", "I'll thrash the Dog I'll box him what Dare to act contrary to the Opinions of of his Spiritual Dictator no not turn in his Temporals. Turn him out", "Turn him out", "CHURCH Millitant", "Unqualified Submission to our Spiritual Guides"

BOXERS of BANGOR or MESSENGERS of PEACE,

Boxers of Bangor or Messengers of Peace was published. The messengers may be both a satirical reference to the violent sentiments of the clergymen and their supporters who threaten to "Thrash the Dog" Grindley for daring to "act contrary to the Opinions of Spiritual Dictation", and a simple description of Mrs Warren's Sabine-like attempts to restrain her apoplectic husband. At the trial the prosecution noted that only "by the intervention of Mrs Warren the bishop was at last quieted from his passion and withdrawn from the riot."[4]

Boxers of Bangor or Messengers of Peace, published by Fores, London, 1796.

In contrast to the earlier print, the "Boxers of Bangor" were not characterised as Welsh, as the seventeenth-century representations of Archbishop John Williams had not combined his portrait with tokens of nationality, despite their ready availability in the period. All the more significant, therefore, are the leeks in the hats of the participants in *A Welch K.t Roasted, and Baisted*. Though the national emblems were not made much of, this seems to be the earliest surviving print in which the political adventures of a Welsh person were linked visually to national stereotype. In the heyday of political satire in English prints, from the 1770s to the 1820s, when individuals from Wales such as the Bishop of Bangor attracted attention, they were generally stereotyped, or at least marked out with a token of Welshness, usually the leek. A case in point is the most frequently represented Welsh man in the period, Sir Watkin Lewes, who was of particular interest to a London audience because of his close association with city politics. Watkin Lewes, born in 1740, was the son of a vicar who had enriched himself greatly by marriage to an heiress with estates in Glamorgan and Pembrokeshire. He practised as a lawyer in London and interested himself in local politics having failed four times to get elected to parliament in Worcester. By 1773 he had been knighted and by 1780 he was Lord Mayor, finally getting into parliament through the back door as one of the city members.

His first appearance in the prints came as a result of his presentation of petitions to parliament in 1771 from the counties of Pembroke, Glamorgan and Carmarthen in support of the imprisoned John Wilkes. The *Oxford Magazine* published a rather benign caricature of him, to be followed on his knighthood by a representation in the lengthy series published by Mat. Darley. Most of these were given the title "Macaroni"[5] and were far from complimentary, but again Sir Watkin got off lightly. From 1781 until 1790 he appeared regularly in caricature groups, his ever expanding girth and national origins marking him out in the crowd, as in

Watkin Lewes Esq. *presenting the Addresses from the Counties of Pembroke, Carmarthen, & Cardigan, to the Lord Mayor Alderman Wilkes, & Alderman Oliver in the Tower .*

Thus Ancient Britons, gen'rous, bold & free,
Untaught at Court to bend the supple Knee,
Corruption's Shrine with honest Pride disdain,
And only bow to Freedom's Patriot Train. *1771*

Chevalier Vatkens Louis,
by Mat. Darley, "Macaroni"
series, 1773.

*Watkin Lewes presenting
the Addresses...,*
published in the *Oxford
Magazine,* 1771.

The City Candidates of 1781, where he rides on a goat in the uniform of the City Militia. Sarcastic reference is made to his previous failures as a parliamentary candidate; "Ye Quakers of Wors'ter Farwell," he remarks. In 1784, he was caricatured as an acolyte of William Pitt—in *Plum Pudding Billy* he is shown presenting his political master with a pudding in which is inserted a large leek. After 1790, Sir Watkin disappeared from the prints. He lost both his fortune and his parliamentary seat and ended his days as a rather privileged inmate of the Fleet Prison, residing in the London Coffee House, under the prison's authority.

Despite Sir Watkin Lewes's vigorous pursual of political advancement in England, he was also an active participant in expatriate Welsh life in London, which no doubt accounts for his particularly close association with the national stereotype in the prints. He was treasurer of the Society of Ancient Britons, to whose favourite national vanity sarcastic reference was made in the 1771 caricature:
     Thus Ancient Britons, gen'rous, bold & free,
     Untaught at Court to bend the supple knee...

The annual Saint David's Day celebrations, to whose Bacchanalian excesses attention had been regularly drawn in the seventeenth century, were still the subject of comment in the late eighteenth century when they were held under the aegis of the societies, the first of which had been the Ancient Britons. *A Feast on St. David's Day* is dated 1 March 1790, and *St. DAVID'S Day, or, The Society of ANCIENT BRITONS going to Dine on RABBITS etc.* is of about the same period and they share a common iconography. The caricatures are probably stereotypical rather than representations of individuals.

The Ancient Britons were, indeed, little more than a social gathering, but the Cymmrodorion Society, founded in 1751, had ambitions to be a focus

A WELSH FEAST ON St DAVID'S DAY.

for Welsh intellectual life, for scholarship and patronage. As we have seen, sixteen years earlier Lewis Morris, one of the founders, was already engaged in attempts to promote printing in Wales. With their energies concentrated in London, the ample opportunities that were presented to the caricaturists by some of their wilder antiquarian fantasies might have been expected to result in a burst of personal satire and some new imagery. In 1770, the second president of the society, Sir Watkin Williams Wynn, son of the subject of the Denbighshire election satires, dressed up as a druid to attend a fancy dress ball. Though the event was noted in the press[6] it did not result in a caricature. However important the intense if sporadic activity of the Cymmrodorion to the development of Welsh culture, intellectual leaders such as the Morris brothers and Evan Evans, Ieuan Fardd, working on texts in the Welsh language, were of little interest to the London public. Their influence on English ideas came about largely through the interpretations of English poets and intellectuals, notably Thomas Gray, and were taken seriously. Gray's poem "The Bard", was inspired by Ieuan Fardd and by the poet's excitement at listening to John Parry, Sir Watkin's harper. As we noted, the visual imagery it inspired from Paul Sandby, Thomas Jones and others, remained the prerogative of academic art. A further factor may have been the increasing vogue for ridiculing the Scots, whose answer to "The Bard", Macpherson's *Ossian*, was under suspicion from the beginning. It was only those Welsh people like Sir Watkin Lewes who combined Welshness (he became a member of the Council of the Cymmrodorion in 1762) with a high political profile, who attracted attention. The other Sir Watkin, a patron of the arts on a lavish scale who relished his ancestry but cut a poor figure politically, made only a few appearances in caricature, most famously in Gillray's *Ancient Music* of 1787. He has a goat's head and sits, grossly overweight, listening to a performance by "The Concert of Ancient Music" (of which he was a founder) in the Tottenham Court Rooms. Gillray's cartoon illustrates Wolcot's "Ode upon Ode", in which Sir Watkin was sarcasticallly described as:

The Sleek Welsh Deity who Music knows—
The Alexander of the Tot'n'am Troops.

Sir Watkin's prodigious girth is evident from a caricature of about 1770 by Thomas Patch.[7] The caricature, clearly labelled as representing Sir Watkin, makes doubtful his traditional identification with a number of other images

A Welsh Feast on St. David's Day, published by W. Holland, London, 1790.

59

of the period. *The Mino Goat* of about 1780 and a Macaroni caricature of 1774, *A WELCH K-T On the look out for a Wife*, clearly illustrate the same gentleman, but his distinctive nose is most unlike that of Patch's Sir Watkin. In any case, Sir Watkin had married his second wife in 1771, and so was presumably not on the look out for another. The meaning of *The Mino Goat*, one of the finest and most complex Welsh satires of the period, unfortunately also remains a mystery. The subject describes himself as:

From Shire Caernarvon, sleet & snow,
From Climes of humble fame,
Where Hips themselves in Hot-beds grow,
A Minogoat I came.

The animal-like Welsh persona of the subject is more aggressively drawn than usual in the period. We are invited to "Come and purchase poor Taff's dainty Cakes, & fine Fruit/Hur will give you Lies, Noise, News & Nonsense to boot." The newspaper boy offers the *Morning Post*, which was founded in 1780, giving an approximate date for the cartoon.[8] In the foreground an astonished goat farts on seeing his human compatriot having sprouted horns. The second verse of the caption recalls the abusive tirades of an earlier period:

From lands where shoes are yet unknown,
Where scabs and drabs smell strong,
Where backs run short, bare bums dark brown,
And heads not over long.

A "drab" in current English vernacular was a whore or a prostitute, but the reference to the length of heads, that is, to the limited intellectual capacity of the Welsh, is more unusual, and may suggest either a Welsh author of

The Mino Goat, by William Austin, c.1780.

the verses or an author very familiar with Welsh talk. *Hirben*—long headed—is a Welsh euphemism for shrewdness.

The only immediately recognisable character in the cartoon is John Wilkes, centre of a lively group drinking in a back room. His iconography in the prints was extensive, reflecting his high political profile and popularity among radical sections of the English public. Wilkes, as we have seen, had a close relationship with the most prominent Welsh satirist of the 1760s and 1770s, Evan Lloyd. The extent to which attitudes to the Welsh had changed may be gauged from the fact that Wilkes was a notorious English xenophobe with a particular detestation for the Scots. Nevertheless, in 1769, one of the newspapers with which his views were closely associated remarked that,"The Welsh and the Scotch, who inhabit the remote ends of this kingdom, are very opposite in their principles. The former are hot, generous, and great lovers of Liberty. The latter are violent and tyrannical."[9]

Lloyd had met Wilkes in 1768, when both were held in the King's Bench prison for libels. According to Lloyd, they had there, "good eating, good drinking, good company, and a very comfortable garden",[10] a situation resulting from Wilkes' celebrity at the time. It was a high point in Evan Lloyd's life and the friendship established there flourished. Wilkes wrote Lloyd's epitaph when he died at the age of 41 in 1776, a premature demise brought on by an excess of drink.[11] The cry "Wilkes and Liberty" had always been an inspiration to Lloyd, who made both the traditional association of liberty with his own nation and an optimistic assessment of the radical views of his compatriots. Writing to Wilkes from Wales in September 1771, he said:

"You have a thousand well wishers among the hills, & I believe the hills themselves, those natural Bulwarks of Liberty, wd rejoice to have its champion among them."[12]

Among Wilkes' thousand liberty-loving Welsh well-wishers were most of Lloyd's circle of emigré intellectuals and visiting gentry of liberal inclination in London. They found themselves welcome at the highest tables. Some fashionable and influential English people were not averse to referring to themselves as Welsh on occasion, in this period. One such was the actor David Garrick,[13] and he was prepared to extend his hospitality to young

Welsh intellectuals and artists. Thomas Jones of Pencerrig, some four years after leaving Wilson's studio, recorded a day trip in the company of another Welsh painter, William Parry (son of John Parry, Sir Watkin's harper), and Evan Lloyd. Thomas Jones's record of the day gives a flavour of the London of the time and of its attractions for the Welsh on the inside track:

"On the 16th (July, 1769) Evan Lloyd the Poet, Charles Hemmings, an old fellow collegian, Parry, late pupil of Reynolds, and my self hired a Coach for the day, dined at the *Toy* at Hampton, and after dinner Lloyd introduced us to Mr Garrick at his elegant Villa there, who very politely shewed the house, attended us round the walks and Shrubberies, and as a particular Compliment, conducted us to his study, a detached Building in the Garden, which being, as he told us, dedicated to Retirement, had only one chair in it—A bottle of Wine was ordered, and standing around his writing desk, The glass was circulated and enlivened with the flippant Conversation of these two Wits, untill a Coach drawing up, announced My Lord Somebody—upon which we took our leave, and returning to the Toy to take another Bottle—concluded the evening together at the Crown and Anchor tavern in the Strand."[14]

The subjects of the sudden flush of caricatures of Welsh people in the second half of the eighteenth century were drawn mainly from Lloyd's circle, rather than from the intellectual leaders of the Cymmrodorion. John Pugh Pryce of Gogerddan, for instance, lampooned in 1770 as *The Merionethshire Macaroni,* was a long-standing friend, and Sir Watkin Lewes was a regular drinking partner, along with Wilkes, at the Crown and Anchor. Evan Lloyd benefitted materially from Sir Watty's rise. On 13 April 1773, he wrote to his father that:

"Yesterday I was up to my Gums in ice-Cream & Jellies at the Mansion

house—to day Sheriff Lewes gives an Entertainment at Joiners' Hall, & I must get ready to attend..."[15]

Lloyd's fondness for the image of the Welsh as the defenders of Liberty was obviously widely shared and bragged about. Sir Watty was mocked for it in the *Morning Post* on the occasion of his enthronement as Lord Mayor in 1780, when he used the beadles with good effect to keep the rabble away from the goings-on:

"Yesterday, Sir Watkin Lewes, the new Lord Mayor, began his annual sovreignty with a striking innovation upon freedom—the great avenue leading from Fleet Street was barred by a temporary railing and a group of beadles and peace officers prevented any from passing to Ludgate Street, except privates. By this means many worthy citizens of Westminster were prevented from seeing the procession of their London freemen, and his Lordship made happy in the compliments of the Court ladies and gentlemen."[16]

Wit and sarcasm of this kind was in fashion, a most highly regarded accomplishment. Occasionally, Evan Lloyd's letters and poems reflect how closely visual satire was integrated into the literature and politics of London—into the very thought of the period. In 1763, five years before they met, the *St James's Chronicle* published verses by Lloyd in support of Wilkes and his party and against Hogarth.[17] The great visual satirist was himself satirized for having sold out to the government who had paid him to ridicule the opposition in a drawing called *The Times*.

Evan Lloyd's imagery was strongly visual, as if he were writing a description of an imagined print. *The Powers of the Pen* contains the lines:

The Merionethshire Macaroni, by Mat. Darley, London, 1772.

Sir Watkin Lewis, perhaps by George Dance, c.1775.

A Welch Tandem, by
James Gillray, published
by Hannah Humphrey,
London, 1801.

Tentanda Via..., by James
Gillray, published by
Hannah Humphrey,
London, 1810.

Perch'd on a Column of *Reviews*
Sits a grave *Owl*, and seems to muse...
An ideot *Ass* gives evidence
By *braying*, of the approach of *Sense*.

Evan Lloyd was a priest, from 1763 the absentee vicar of Llanfair Dyffryn Clwyd. On his visits from London to his home near Y Bala, generally in the winter, he was in the habit of drinking at the Hywel Dda tavern on the road to Dolgellau. He and his friends called themselves the Lunatick Club because they met at the full moon, by the light of which they could stumble home in an inebriated condition in comparative safety. Their meetings were in the style of tavern eisteddfodau, with poetising and singing accompanying the drink. Some of Lloyd's friends would certainly have frequented the somewhat more formal eisteddfodau revived with sponsorship from the Gwyneddigion Society a few years later, though Lloyd had drunk himself to death by that time. In 1789 there were two such meetings. The first, at Corwen, gave rise to a celebrated dispute on the relative poetical virtues of Thomas Edwards, Twm o'r Nant, Jonathan Hughes and Walter Davies, Gwallter Mechain. The adjudication was left to the Gwyneddigion in London who came down on the side of Gwallter Mechain. Tempers became frayed and "Dr. D Samwel proceeded so far as to demand satisfaction of one of the opponents of Twm o'r Nant." Soon after, at the Bala meeting, Thomas Jones, an excise officer at Corwen and one of the organisers of the two events, "through a whim, produced and hung, in the assembly room, an emblematical painting, representing, on one side the Muse in tears, the other depicting 'The sense and thoughts of Jonathan Hughes,' 'The Muse and flowing vein of Thomas Edwards,' 'The rules and purity of language of Walter Davies.'"[18] Clearly, this lost painting was firmly rooted in the tradition of the satirical prints.

Such events were not frequented by Methodists who expended much energy in trying to rid the country of drink and harps in this period of the

64

movement. Evan Lloyd and his friends harboured an intense dislike of such Puritanism, and they attacked the Great Revival. Although Methodism was also an important issue in England, the power of the revival and the particularity of its characteristics in Wales provided the only suggestion of a contemporary Welsh focus in their work. The ideal British race, in its pure and innocent state as depicted in Lloyd's poem *The Curate* of 1776, was manifesting less than ideal characteristics. Rice Jones, one of Lloyd's drinking partners in the Lunatick Club, wrote a fierce attack on the increasing influence of the Methodists:

> To the poor they come unbidden—sly
>   Steal away the women:
>   Ranting, jumping the night long,
>   Bewitched, bewildered throng.[19]

That Methodism alone scratched the surface of their Anglophilia is of great significance since this was the emergence of a modern movement, distinct to Wales. It was the stirring of a world of ideas perceived from within that was profoundly reshaping the nation, leaving the world of Evan Lloyd, important as it must have seemed at the time, on the margins.

It was for a libel in his satire *The Methodist* that Evan Lloyd went to prison. William Price of Rhiwlas, a member of the Cymmrodorion, took himself to be Libidinoso, one of Satan's more hypocritical agents in the north:

> When in a dark, romantic Wood,
> In which an antique Mansion stood,
> He spied, close to a Hovel-door
> A *saint* conversing with his Whore:
> Double he seem'd, and worn with Age,
> Little adapted to engage,
> In *Love's* hot War...

Price's suit resulted not only in Lloyd's pleasurable imprisonment, but also in a less agreeable fine of £50 handed down by Lord Mansfield.

Not surprisingly, despite his anti-Methodism, Lloyd's *risqué* literary activities did little for his advancement in the church—advancement which, it must be said, was largely of interest to him because of its pecuniary implications. In the light both of the libel and an attack in *The Curate* on the bishops, he was refused advancement by Dr Shipley, absentee Bishop of St Asaph:

> He in Christ's doctrine deals, by way of trade.
> Money by *preaching Poverty* is made...

His friends were told that "Mr Lloyd would have to perform quarantine".[20]

After the death of Lloyd and the decline of his drinking partner, Sir Watty, the most politically active of the Welsh in London was Sir Watkin Williams Wynn, son of the great connoisseur. Like his father, he was president of the Cymmrodorion, but also had—along with Charles, one of his brothers—a high political profile. As a result they featured in a number of prints, though the earliest of them, the delightful *Welch Tandem*, 1801, by Gillray, does not seem to have been occasioned by any political misadventure. A *Welch Tandem* also features the third brother, Henry, and the traditional farting goat, one of a group of undisciplined steeds (symbolic of a Welsh rabble) hauling the chariot in the direction of Wynnstay. Gillray himself was obviously pleased by this image, since he repeated it in his large and complex *Tentanda Via* of 1810. The print has Lord Grenville, uncle of the Wynn brothers, showering favours from a hot air balloon. Unfortunately, despite this connection, the brothers' expect-ations were not always realised, a situation satirised in *More Pigs than Teats* of 1806, in which the porcine Wynns have failed to squeeze their way through to the sow in the rush for advancement. Charles Watkin Williams Wynn's political ambitions in particular were a soft target for the satirists since he possessed an unusually high-pitched voice. He and his elder brother were known in the corridors of power as "Bubble and Squeak", an appellation to which Gillray refers in a poster on the wall in his satire on Prime Minister Fox and Grenville, who reputedly held sway over him, *The Bear and his Leader*, also of 1806. Unfortunately, Charles'

Monstrosities of 1799.—
Scene, Kensington
Gardens, by James
Gillray, London, 1799,
detail.

Despair, by James Gillray,
London, 1802.

particular ambition was to become Speaker of the House of Commons. It was supposed that should he succeed in gaining that office he would be addressed as "Mr Squeaker".

Among Sir Watkin's *fin de siècle* compatriots, only a few achieved the doubtful distinction of being caricatured in London. The independent-minded politics of Tyrwhitt-Jones of Carreghova, Member of Parliament for Denbighshire, had him caricatured regularly, though as in *Despair* of 1802, he is characterised more as a redneck than as a Welsh person. Thomas Johnes of Hafod, on the other hand, was a sophisticated aesthete with little taste for politics and like the second Sir Watkin, did not figure largely in the prints, despite his considerable celebrity amongst the English intelligentsia. Only one caricature of him has survived, Gillray's *Monstrosities of 1799*, in which the written allusion is very oblique. A footnote reads "for the Origin of the Word consult the J o h n n e s.onian Dictionary..." Phillip Yorke of Erddig's penchant for theatricals involving his extensive household was satirised in *Dilettanti Theatricals:—or—a Peep at the Green Room.*

The most frequently caricatured Welsh person in the period was not Welsh at all. The amours of the Prince of Wales, the future George IV, were of particular interest to the London satirists. In *Taffy and Hur Wife Shentleman of Wales,* 1786, the prince gallops past a signpost to Wynnstay on a huge goat. Both caption and image draw on the long tradition of Welsh satirical imagery, including the suggestion that Welsh women were bold and immoral. The Prince's mistress, Mrs Fitzherbert, rides with a particularly vulgar posture, and a footnote records that "The Welch women all ride cross-legged and bare-backed." The reference to Wynnstay is obscure if it is not simply that Wynnstay is synonymous with Wales. Despite his tenuous connection with the nation, the Welsh iconography of prints involving the Prince was sometimes complex. In *Enchantments lately seen upon the Mountains of Wales,—or—Shon-ap-Morgan's Reconcilement to the Fairy Princess,* 1796, it reaches high fantasy. The Prince, as in several other cartoons, is a fat goat, connoting not only his Welsh connection but also his libido. Grotesquely, he embraces his wife in reconciliation on top of a mountain. On another peak, those who have brokered the reconciliation dance for joy—Lord Loughborough, the Duke of York and Lord Cholmondly. However, Lady Jersey, the prince's late mistress, staggers backwards in shock, and her husband, also a goat, is about to follow her into the abyss, frightened by a voice from on high: "What? What? What?", was the King's favourite expression.

TAFFY AND HUR WIFE, SHENTLEMAN OF WALES.

ENCHANTMENTS lately seen upon the Mountains of WALES, — or — Sharp-Mayani Reconcilement to the Fairy Princess.

There are numerous other examples. The unmerciful satirising of the future king by his own people, making extensive use of the ancient anti-Welsh iconography, was in marked contrast to the treatment he received from the everloyal Welsh. As we have seen, his first appearance in a print of Welsh origin was Hugh Hughes's *The Landing of His Majesty, George the Fourth, at Holyhead, August 7th, 1821*, which was coupled with a detailed account of the "indescribable joy" felt by the inhabitants of Anglesey on the King's condescension at visiting the country. The King, who had somewhat reluctantly[21] called in at Holyhead on his way to Ireland, stayed the night with the Marquess of Anglesey. On his return from Ireland he landed at Milford Haven, apparently intending to visit Wynnstay to make a rendezvous. "The Chief of Wynnstay intends to summon the bards and minstrels (as in the days of yore) to give our beloved Monarch a specimen of the manner in which the Antient Britons performed their national music," remarked the *Court Newsman* with mild sarcasm. It was this aspect of the King's Welsh excursion that attracted attention in London. In *Taffy's Honor at Stake* the front of Wynnstay is accurately

Taffy and Hur Wife, Shentleman of Wales, published by Fores, London, 1786.

Enchantments lately seen upon the Mountains of Wales..., by James Gillray, published by Hannah Humphrey, London, 1796.

WALES

WHO SAYS A WELSHMAN IS LIKE A BILLY GOAT

shown with Sir Watkin refusing entrance to Lady Conyngham, the King's latest mistress, who has arrived for the party. "Porter! Shut all W——s out!!", he shouts, despite the lady's protestation that she belongs to the family (that is, she is not a whore). The King, newly arrived in a coach, is deprived of his sport by Sir Watkin's high principles, and drives off, frustrated.

The main thrust of the prints made with the intaglio processes was personal caricature. Nevertheless, some stereotypes illustrating the supposed culture characteristics of the nation were produced in the new medium. They show little iconographic development from the seventeenth-century woodcut tradition, though the texts became reduced to extended captions. The Welsh person's addiction to ancestry was regularly lampooned. *The Welch Traveller*, advertised by Laurie & Whittle in 1795 as being suitable for sale by country booksellers, was indeed somewhat out of the London mainstream, which is represented more accurately by a contemporary print by Richard Newton entitled *On a Journey to a Courtship in Wales*. The Welch Traveller rides on a horse rather than a goat and mysteriously carries onions rather than leeks and cheese.[22] However, the thrust of the two prints is the same. The Traveller gives his ancestry precisely to the ninth generation to an innkeeper who merely wishes to know his name, while the grotesque bridegroom's servant carries his master's "Pedigree before the Flood". A third example of the genre, one of a series called *Sketches of National Character*, subtly brings out the animal characteristics often displayed grossly in the personal satires of the period such as *The Mino Goat* and the *Enchantments...* Although David Jones, clutching his extensive pedigree extending back before the creation of the world, does not ride on a goat, his facial features have taken on a distinctly goat-like quality. "Who says a Welshman's like a Billy Goat?" he asks, innocently.

Nevertheless, the predominant characteristics of the late eighteenth-century Welsh person remained stupidity and poverty. Stupidity, as we have seen, was related to the Welsh immigrant's difficulty with the English language, satirised directly in *The Welch Sailor's Mistake or Tars in Conversation*, where David, on board a ship, crucially mistakes a leak for a leek: "A ferry coot fetchitable it is. I should have liked to have had a pit with you." As far as the dweller in the metropolis is concerned, stupidity is an

attribute of almost any rural outsider, and the redneck or country bumpkin Welsh appear regularly. This may reflect the decay of the idea of Wales as foreign and of the people as potentially troublesome, to be replaced by a notion of its being "in the country". It certainly became conventional for the Welsh in London to refer to a trip home as "going to the country" by the 1820s. In *The Radnorshire Christening*, 1802, the country wife is the target, having forgotten to bring the baby, and in *A Welch Justice*, it is the local JP:

"Look you coot woman, all you say may be fery true—but hur makes it a rule never to hear put *one side of the question*—for if hur hears poth; it pothers hur poor prains, in such a manner hur does not know what hur is apout."

The poverty of the Welsh, previously represented by Poor Taff, the down-at-heel gentleman, became in the later eighteenth century more commonly associated with the clergy. Handing down his hefty fine, Lord Mansfield referred disparagingly to Evan Lloyd as "the Welsh parson". In 1773, the same derisory epithet was employed in the title of *A Whipping*

The Welch Traveller, published by Laurie and Whittle, London, 1801.

The Welch Sailor's Mistake..., engraved by Rowlandson after G.M.Woodward, published by Tegg, London, c.1808.

69

for the Welsh Parson, in which Scriblerius Flagellarius satirised the satirist. The poverty of the parson was proverbial in England as early as Chaucer, but the particular association with Wales came much later. Bowles' and Carver's print The Welch Curate is unlikely to be older than 1766 and seems to be the earliest surviving visual reference of the sort. It may be that Evan Lloyd was the first to attract the epithet, and that Lord Mansfield's use of it in 1768, even if he did not invent it, was the cause of its popularisation. Certainly the expression was not without a substantial basis in reality. The livings were often very poor even when not further impoverished by supporting absentee parsons (such as Lloyd) who generally employed a curate for a pittance to do their work for them. The Welch Curate portrays his miserable condition. It is more a mildly amusing and sympathetic description than a satire. The young curate, whose wife is out earning some cash by washing, prepares dinner, studies the Bible, listens to his son's lessons and rocks the cradle with his toe, all at the same time. The Welch Parson of 1790 by G.M. Woodward, is also not as unsympathetic as it might appear out of the context of the group of prints from which it is taken. They are a parody on the Ages of Man theme, also popular in the prints, but satirising the hierarchical structure of the English church. Others include the Priest and the Pedagogue, but bottom of the pile is the Welch Parson:

> Best Scene of all
> With which I close this reverend description,
> Is your Welch Parson, with his noble living,
> Sans shoes, sans hose, sans breeches, sans everything.

Towards the end of the eighteenth century, increasing numbers of individual prints in series, and multi-image prints, brought together stereotypes of the nationalities of Britain, reflecting growing English nationalism and self-confidence in the loyalty of a unified Britain under

St. David for Wales, published by Carington Bowles, London, 1781.

English domination. One of the finest series, based on the patron saints of the nations, was published by Carington Bowles. *St David for Wales* is a complex collection of Welsh symbols, based on Poor Taff and bound together and framed by pillars made of leeks with goat's heads for capitals. In addition to his seventeenth-century leeks, cheese (nibbled by mice) and herrings, he has now acquired a harp, and a suggestion that his nineteenth-century stereotypical penchant for song is in the making:

> The Glorious Ancient British Saint Behold,
> David the Great in Fames Records Inroll'd.
> Loaded with Grand Repast his Sons to Treat
> And sets before them fine Welch Ale & Meat
> Herrings, Leeks, Black Puddings, Mustard, toasted Cheese
> With Goats Milk, Butter & such food as these
> Then brings his Minstrells Harp of graceful sound
> Whose Musick cheers their Hearts & makes their Voice Resound.

After Sir Watkin Williams Wynn's harper, John Parry, had attracted the attention of the intelligentsia in England in the 1750s, the increasing number of people who toured Wales itself had been pleased to find a blind harper awaiting them (and their cash) in many inns. Among them was Edward Jones of Llangollen who was able to take advantage of good family connections:

"Breakfast was announced by the Harper of the Inn commencing his Performance; his name is Edward Jones, first Cousin to the Prince of Wales' Harper, an excellent Performer and good Musician, although Blind and by Trade a Shoe-Maker; he is besides an ingenious Mechanic, the custom is for visitors to contribute upon quitting the Inn Money as a Reward for his Labour..."[23]

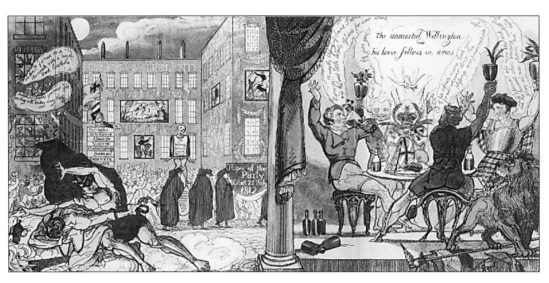

72

A Welch Wedding and *An Irish Fortune Hunters Wedding*, by Richard Newton, London, c.1795.

Effects of the Arrival of French Eagles, by W.H. Brooke, London, 1812.

His cousin of the same name had published his famous *Musical and Poetical Relicks of the Welsh Bards* in 1784. The second edition contained de Loutherbourg's celebrated engraving of *The Last Bard*, clutching his harp. By the end of the century, the bardic revival which it celebrated was beginning to be reflected in the popular prints, though it developed too late to be used in the caricature of individuals in the great age of English satire. A harper of a more realistic kind, as recorded in the drawings of Ibbotson, Turner and many lesser English painters, appeared in a national stereotype caricature of the late eighteenth century, linked to a companion Irish image. In *A Welch Wedding*, a grotesque country parson, presumably the bridegroom, dances energetically with an ample-bosomed bride who is already *déshabillé*. They are contrasted with *An Irish Fortune Hunter's Wedding*, or rather proposal, also accompanied by national music.

Such grotesque Welsh and Irish stereotypes, along with their Scottish equivalent, underwent a revealing metamorphosis during the French wars when the threat of invasion preyed on English minds. The poverty-stricken, stupid and cowardly Welsh were suddenly perceived by English cartoonists to be loyal, sturdy and brave, and the object of brotherly love and affection. In *Thoughts on Invasion*, a massive John Bull is stoutly defended by soldiers of the four nations ranged along the coast facing the devil Napoleon. Similarly, *The Loyalists Alphabet* has 24 small lettered vignettes, of which "M" stands for "MAGNA Charta's strong chain"—a chain formed by a Welshman, a Scotsman, an Irishman and an Englishman, linking hands in a display of loyal equality. In 1797, the English cartoonists had had particularly good reason to change their attitude to the Welsh, when a French invasion force landed near Fishguard under their American commander, Colonel Tate. Their intention had not been conquest, but to frighten the population and the government in order to

Py St. DAVID.— they took the Womens red Cloaks for Soldiers & look'd
as pale as the Tiffel himself.— Set 'em come.— whose afraid.— WELCH
POYS.— reaping hooks.— toasted cheese.— ..... creen Leaks and Little
FISHGUARD for ever.!

A FISHGUARD FENCIBLE.

London. Published as the Act directs March 1797. by G. M. Woodward Berners Street.

facilitate an intended assault on Ireland. The landing succeeded in
creating panic as far away as Liverpool, but the victory of Lord Cawdor's
militia, and the famous exploit of the local women and their leader Jemima
Nicholas, entered the folklore of the nation. John Mends of Haverfordwest
explained the French decision to surrender as follows:

A Fishguard Fencible,
published by G.M.
Woodward, London,
1797.

"The cause was owing to the vigilance, alackrity and spirit of the Welch,
who came running from all Quarters of the Country to oppose them, and in
about 48 hours they amounted to 7 or 8 thousand men of all sorts, some
well armed, others with long pike staffs, others with sythes straitined—a
Desperate weapon—others with pitchforks, and, above all, about 400
poor women with Red Flanel over their shoulders, whom the French at
Distance took for soldiers, as they appeared all red."

The event was celebrated in ballads and in a fine naive painting, but
although several cartoons of the period show heroic yokels armed with
pitchforks repelling the enemy, only one refers specifically to the invasion,
entitled *A Fishguard Fencible*. It combines the ancient tradition of
Wenglish and the leek with the Welsh country bumpkin of recent origin:
"Py St. DAVID—they took the Womens red Cloaks for Soldiers & look'd as
pale as the Tiffel himself... reaping hooks—toasted cheese—creen Leaks
and Little FISHGUARD for ever!", he says.

The most complex example of this genre was *Effects of the Arrival of
French Eagles*, of 1812. On the left half of the print, the dire effects on
London of a French invasion are illustrated, while on the right, four national
characters toast the hero of the hour. "Cot of his infinite mercy look you for
ever shower down his plessings and preservations upon... the immortal
Wellington and his brave fellows in arms," incants the loyal Welshman,
echoing Shakespeare's Fluellin, two hundred years before.

73

The Modern Toilet

IV Welsh satirists in the English world

The London-oriented intellectual class of the eighteenth century, with only a cursory glance over its shoulder in the direction of the Methodist wind of change, found little to say to the outside world of Wales itself. Beyond the projection of the people as Ancient Britons, the shortcomings of the established church and election scandals were the only obvious manifestations of contemporary British life in Wales which merited attention in England. Not surprisingly, therefore, it was the activities of a clergyman which provided the material for the first substantial venture in visual political satire to emerge from Wales itself. The pioneer in this, as in many other things, was Thomas Pennant of Downing, in Flintshire. Like most of his contemporaries amongst the gentry and the intellectuals of the London societies, Methodism troubled him, but unlike Evan Lloyd, Pennant was a Tory squire. Despite his enquiring mind and a general inclination to toleration and fairness, he was very much opposed to disturbance of the established order, whether that disturbance emanated from "fanatical Methodist preachers"[1] or libertarian activists such as Lloyd's friend Wilkes.

Thomas Pennant's first venture into the prints was a social rather than a political satire, but nonetheless conservative in tone and a reaction against the libertarian atmosphere of the period. *Camber's Letter to John Bull* was "A ridicule on the bold and masculine fashion of the Ladies wearing riding habits all times of the day." The kind of polarised and exclusive sexual roles proposed as the ideal by Rousseau were beginning to be questioned, one manifestation of which was a fashion among some radically-minded women for cross dressing. Pennant's letter, originally sent to a newspaper, was republished by Staton in 1781 with an engraving as *Modern Toilet*. Pennant retained both an original sketch of the idea, presumably prepared to his own instructions, and a coloured drawing on which the finished print was based. The drawings may be the work of his resident artist, Moses Griffith, since the careful and unflamboyant technique is unusual in the period and unlike the work of a London caricaturist. Griffiths might also have engraved the print, though it is more likely that the drawings were sent to Chester or to London to be copied.

Pennant's second venture into the prints was very different from the *Modern Toilet*, stimulated by the activities of the clergyman whom he would pursue obsessively for many years. In 1782, William Shipley, Dean of Saint Asaph, had paid for the publication of a tract on political freedom written by William Jones, his brother-in-law. William Jones was one of those Englishmen of Welsh descent who were pleased to make the association between the land of their fathers and the idea of freedom. Indeed, as a circuit judge in the south-west, Jones had distinguished himself by the practical application of his principles, giving important support to Wales through his opposition to Burke's plan to remove all Welsh cases to London. He was well known to Pennant, who, despite his dislike of his politics, had sent him an autograph copy of one of his books. The republication of Jones's *Principles of Government, in a Dialogue between a Gentleman and a Farmer* by Shipley resulted in the Dean's indictment for seditious libel. The case stimulated the production of four cartoons by Pennant, who took a dim view of Shipley's libertarian inclinations. These are the earliest political cartoons which have both a Welsh context and a Welsh designer.

The case also gave rise to the earliest political squib in the Welsh language, though it supported Pennant's enemy, the Dean. It takes the form of an Interlude in which is incorporated William Jones's original text as a conversation between the Fool and the Miser. However, *BARN ar egwyddorion llywodraeth* (An Opinion of the Principles of Government) expands much beyond this core to tell the story of the several trials of the case, recounted by "Hanesydd" (Historian). Pennant's anti-Shipley party were much satirized by the anonymous author, probably Twm o'r Nant, who drew on English-language verbatim accounts of the trials, published at the time as pamphlets, for his information.

Pennant's mildly reforming inclinations led him to conclude that the removal of the worst abuses of church and state power would be the best way to secure the essentials of the *status quo*. In pursuit of moderate

Modern Toilet. Camber's Letter to John Bull, after Thomas Pennant, published by Staton, 1781.

Modern Toilet, early drawing, after Thomas Pennant, c.1781.

Modern Toilet, final drawing, after Thomas Pennant, c.1781.

Thomas Pennant as a child, attributed to Joseph Highmore, c.1738.

The Flintshire Whirlegig, drawn by Francis Grose after Thomas Pennant, c.1784.

reform through petitioning the government, he had crossed swords with the Dean of Saint Asaph as early as 1779:

"The clamors raised in the year 1779, and the apparent discontents grew to such a height, that I thought it prudent that the county of *Flint* should add its weight to the petition, so that by prevailing on government to lessen every unnecessary burden, the minds of the people might be eased, and all ill consequences prevented, for civil war almost threatened."[2]

Pennant, who "at all time professed (his) abhorrence of committees and associations" called an informal meeting which was usurped by Dean Shipley, "burning after the glory of chairman of a committee, and backed by friends he brought with him." To Pennant's irritation, the County Committee for Flint was established, a body of more strongly reforming sentiment than he had envisaged. Pennant's self-confidence deserted him in the meeting. He had "formed a speech which I had not courage enough to speak," he recalled, and so he had it printed instead.

When, in 1782, Shipley received a copy of his brother-in-law's reforming tract, he set it before the committee who approved it, and he decided to have it translated into Welsh. Being advised by more cautious individuals that its contents might do him no good by stirring up the populace, he desisted, but nevertheless, the county Tories led by the Sheriff, the Honourable Thomas Fitzmaurice, attacked him in a meeting on 7 January, 1783. Taking umbrage, Shipley promptly had copies of the pamphlet printed by Marsh in Wrexham, with an explanatory "advertisement", and a few copies were circulated. Fitzmaurice decided to pursue the matter, and failing to get the Treasury to prosecute, did so himself through his attorney, William Jones of Ruthin. According to Pennant's account, Shipley "imprudently published a little pamphlet which subjected him to a prosecution by the Honourable Thomas Fitzmaurice. I listed under the banner of the last, whom I thought very ill used by the county gentlemen; they ow'd him numberless obligations, yet suddenly veer'd about to the other side. Their inconsistency was satirised in a small print most unintelligibly engraven."

No copy of this unsatisfactory print seems to have survived, but it was later redrawn by one of Pennant's many artist acquaintances, Francis Grose,[3]

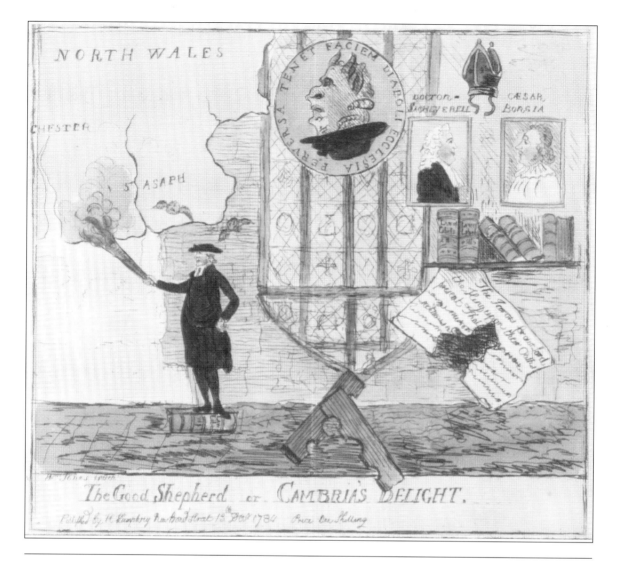

The Good Shepherd, or Cambria's Delight, engraved by Sawyer after Thomas Pennant, published by Hannah Humphrey, 1784.

"with many expressions of humour". The drawing, showing several gentlemen turning like a whirligig, has survived. As well as the absentee Bishop of Saint Asaph, the Dean's father, who has lost his mitre, those satirised are presumably the gentlemen who stood as character witnesses for the Dean at his subsequent trial in 1784, that is, Sir Roger Mostyn, Major Williams, Colonel Myddleton, Bennet Williams, and most surprisingly of all, Sir Watkin Williams Wynn.

Shipley was originally indicted for seditious libel at Wrexham Great Sessions. It was a high-profile affair, turning on questions of the liberty of the citizen to express political opinion. The Dean was represented by the great English attorney Erskine, and the proceedings were published by the Society for Constitutional Information with which the author of the original pamphlet, William Jones, was closely associated. The case went from Wrexham to the King's Bench and eventually for trial at Shrewsbury, where, after some wrangling with the judge about the exact wording of a most unusual verdict, the jury found Shipley "guilty of publishing, but whether a libel or not, the jury do not find."[4] Erskine argued for a retrial which was refused, and then for arrest of judgement since no part of the publication had been found criminal. His plea was accepted and Shipley was discharged. As a result of the legal confusion surrounding the protracted proceedings, Fox's government passed the Libel Act in 1792, regarded as having "completed the freedom of the press in this country."[5]

Pennant's first response to these events, in early December, 1784, was to send "to the celebrated political caricaturist Mr Sawyer a design for a... print which he published highly improved under the title the Good Shepherd or Cambria's delight." We see that, as in the case of Hogarth, on some occasions the cartoonist was more of a political mercenary than a person of principle. Pennant's design has been interpreted by Dorothy George:

77

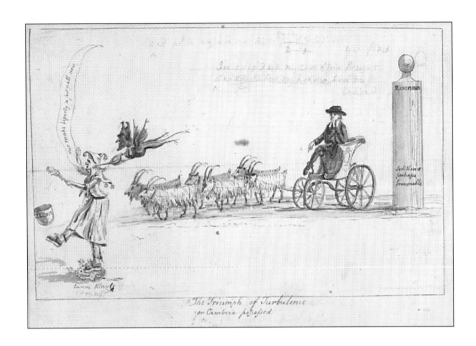

The Triumph of Turbulence or Cambria possessed

*The Triumph of
Turbulence or Mother
Cambria Possessed,*
drawing, c.1784-5, after
Thomas Pennant.

"In *The Good Shepherd or Cambria's Delight*... the Dean stands in the ruins of his cathedral, about to set fire to a map of North Wales using the 'libel' as a firebrand. The large medallion on the window is an adaption of the Pope-Devil double-headed token, used by Protestant reformers in Germany, Holland, and Switzerland in the sixteenth century, from which the inscription, *Ecclesia perversa tenet faciem Diaboli* is literally taken. The place of the Pope is taken by Shipley, who, conjoined with the Devil, has turned the church upside down. He stands on the 'Law of Libel' because the legal argument in the case had turned on the function of the jury in trials for libel."[6]

Although it was indeed a church window that was inverted in the print, the general ruination suggests that Pennant's warning was of the whole world turned upside down, rather than simply the church—that is, of revolution, ignited by William Jones's pamphlet and others like it. The sophisticated references to continental symbolism underline Pennant's erudition and his familiarity with Germany and Switzerland, where he had travelled, drawing the mountain scenery, with Moses Griffith.

Following his acquittal, Dean Shipley had visited his father near Twyford before returning in triumph to St Asaph through Shrewsbury, Wrexham and Ruthin where bonfires were lit and crowds turned out to cheer him. The author of the interlude, *BARN ar egwyddorion llywodraeth*, reported that "the men of the town pulled his carriage in place of the horses, and the valley echoed with rejoicing and victory."

A correspondent to the *Chester Chronicle* chose to report a rather different aspect of the proceedings, suggesting that on 7 January, 1785, a hired mob had had to be restrained from throwing the Dean over Ruthin bridge. Pennant, who was on good terms with the editor of the *Chester Chronicle*, may well have been "Veritas", one of the two correspondents whose differing versions of the events enlivened the paper's columns. He reported that:

"The dean escaped by a blunder in the indictment, not by an honourable acquital. There was the most indecent rejoicings on the occasion in several places in Flintshire. This gave occasion to a print called the *Triumph of Turbulence or Mother Cambria Possessed*. In the background

78

The Triumph of
Turbulence or Mother
Cambria Possessed, after
Thomas Pennant, 1785.

are represented the clergy of St Asaph blowing up poor Mr Fitzmaurice on the church yard wall: the pillar alludes to Lord Mansfield's opinion of the nature of pamphlets."

Lord Mansfield, it will be remembered from his treatment of Evan Lloyd, was no libertarian. He had given the final judgement in the affair.

Like the *Modern Toilet*, the *Triumph of Turbulence* is unusual in its formal qualities. It is quite unlike the work of a professional cartoonist in the period, such as Sawyer or Pennant's friend Grose. Although he does not specifically say so, Pennant must have been its designer, and a preparatory drawing with an early version of both imagery and text, by the same hand, were in Pennant's posession at his death. The final version may have been drawn by Moses Griffith or by one P. Clough of Denbigh who signed a drawing identical to the print in 1785.[7]

Against the background of the Clwydian Hills, the crowd that had drawn the Dean's carriage are represented by a team of unruly goats who, according to the clergyman's lines in the text, he has blinded—that is to say, deceived. There is a broken shackle around his ankle. The revolutionary inclinations of the Welsh proletariat, somewhat unrealistically conjured up in Pennant's conservative imagination, say—in best Wenglish—"Liperty is her foot-pall now". They are embodied in Mother Cambria who tramples on "Tamm Kingss & Crouns" and gives a liberty cap a good kick. The devil Dean blows a seditious blast of presumably hot air into Mother Cambria's ear. This is the earliest home-grown personification of Wales and a complete departure from Poor Taff, the male stereotype of the English popular press. Mother Cambria would be followed by Dame Venodotia, alias Modryb Gwen, the invention of Hugh Hughes, and ultimately by Dame Wales, the character created by J.M. Staniforth for the *Western Mail* at the end of the nineteenth century.

Pennant gave no clue in his writings as to why he chose to personify Wales as a woman, but he may have had Katheryn of Berain in the back of his mind. Katheryn (1534/5-1591) was known as *Mam Cymru* (The Mother of Wales) because so many prominent families were descended from her four marriages. In the eighteenth century she was a well established part of national folklore, having been celebrated by a

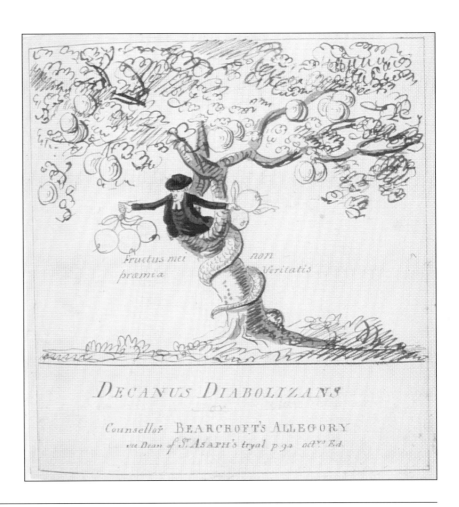

DECANUS DIABOLIZANS

Counsellor BEARCROFT'S ALLEGORY
see Dean of St Asaph's tryal p.91 octavo Ed.

Decanus Diabolizans or Counsellor Bearcroft's Allegory, after Thomas Pennant, c.1785.

succession of famous poets. Katheryn was of particular interest to Pennant since she was a native of Denbighshire. He had Moses Griffith copy a number of genuine and supposed portraits of her, hanging in the houses he visited on his tours. Nevertheless, it must be said that if Pennant's imagination was stimulated by his familiarity with Katheryn, the idea was no more than that of a mother of Wales rather than of a father, since the demented Mother Cambria of the cartoon dances on the crown and Katheryn was of royal descent.

The print was published in February 1785, the dates "23rd & 24th Dec.1784" referring to the turbulent events described.

Thomas Pennant's pursuit of Shipley in the prints was relentless:

"I also caused a drawing to be designed on a comparison made on the Dean's tryal by that eminent lawyer Mr Bearcroft between the grand tempter and the Dean of St Asaph. The first is placed twined round the tree of life offering fine apples allegorical of as many livings accidentally given about the time to the friends of as many gentlemen who swore for him on his tryal all by Shrewsbury clock."

These are the gentlemen turning in the wind in the earlier and unpublished satire, the reason for their unholy alliance with the Dean exposed. Despite his reforming zeal, Dean Shipley, like his father (who had refused advancement to Evan Lloyd), was a notorious pluralist and dispenser of places. This must have seemed to many people a fine irony, truly the world turned upside down, since his Tory protagonist, Pennant, had publicly opposed such abuses in the church. To Pennant's way of thinking it was blatant hypocrisy, and coupled with the personal reversal he had suffered at the hands of the Dean in 1779, probably had as much to do with his espousal of moderate reform as his exaggerated fears of Wales becoming a hotbed of revolution. Pennant was still discussing the possibility of reopening the case against the Dean in 1796. This mixture of high-mindedness and personal vendetta underlies another of his caricatures, known in three versions. *The Cries of the Curates or the Growing Evil* is the earliest, dated 10 March 1783, followed by two slightly different forms

A
FUNERAL SERMON
Preached by the Minifter of
Glangothan, in WALES.

Tearly Pelovad,

I AM come here among you to make a creat preachment upon that dead pody: My text is in the ten and twentieth chapter of the *Maccabees*, te ferfe indeet I cannot now fery well remember, but I am fure it is dere, te vords be defe; *Fecbilate de Orate*, dat is to fhay, Vatch and Pray: And I will ftick to my text, I will warrant you.——Our creat crandfather Adam was a fery coot man, in coot truth w s he, and twelt in Cot's own houfe in Paratife, and a prave place I will warrant you it was; he had efry thing profided to his hand, he did not puy to much as a noggen, piggen, or a fpoon; he had pelofet apple-trees, plumb-trees, pear-trees, fherry-trees, and cotling-trees, and all forts of trees, but for want of coot take heed, he was fallen; ah! how was he fallen? why I will tell you how he was fallen.——Our creat crandmother Eve (a pox and Cot take her for a plaguy paggage) muft go a rambling and a changling from home, and cout not ftay at home with her own hofband, but did rop an orchard, the Devil fhow't the way (for if dere be any mifchief apout the Devil and Women muft have a finger in the pye) fo we came home, and perfuaded her hufpand to eat fome of her ftolen apple; it was creat mercy of Cot it did not ftick in hur throat and choak him.——After dis fhe proft with-child, and was bront to-ped of a fine poy, and call't his name —I cannot now fery well remember—oh. tear! it vas Cain; ay, Cain vas it; he was a prave lat, but an unluck roguey like his mother. And another little time after dat fhe profed with-child again, and was prout to-ped of another prave poy, and called his name Apel; dis vas a fery coot lat, for he did ftick to part of my text, he did pray; and had he vach'd too, before Cot his broder Cain had never come behind his pack and knockt out his prains. Dis vas a murdering fillain, fo he vas op't ed to overun his country, and got him a wife

in a ftrange land, which taught him ftrange tricks I warrant you.——Thus you fee, peloved, how the fins of Ropery and Murder came on the earth, and prout a heavy fhudgment upon the world; wat you think that vas? I will tell you, it proofed thefe patcel of plaguy lawyers, attorneys, and pum-pailifts, to rop the people, and keep their eftates and mo ey all themfelves.——But after di; there came anoder fin upon the earth, and prout a heavier fhudgment upon all the world; vat you tink dat vas? I will tell you, it was the fin of trunkennefs; for Cot's fake beware trinking too much, for our creat crandfader Noah had no fooner fcaped fcowering in de ark, and got fafe to land again, but he went to the firft alehoufe he could find, and there he fat trink trink all day long and all night, and then came home fo trunk and abufed his family.——The fin of trunkennefs, peloved, prought a heavier fhudgment than all the reft; and what a plaguy fhudgment do you think it proofed? why I will tell you, it prout thefe deftroying locufts, thefe confuming catterpillars, thofe hellifh vermin, thofe curfed Egyptian plagues join'd all together, excifemen, and cuftom-houfe officers, to pry into efery nook, and poke for efery drop of coot trink, Cot confound them all, and from theIn *libra nos dominos*, that is to fay, Lort deliver us.— In the treadful day of fhudgment, when the paftors fhall be called to give an account of the fheep delivered to their charge, and I your poor unworthy parfon of *Glangothan* fhell be called to give an account of the fheep delivered to my charge, and when the Lort calls I will fpeak, and when he calls a fecond time I will not anfwer; put when he calls a third time, I will fay as old Eli bid Samuel, " On fay, Lort, for thy fervant heareth;" and when he afketh for the fheep delivered unto my charge, before Cot, I will tell him flat and plain, You are all turned Goats. *Amen.*

Glangothan : Printed for *Sben-ap-Morgan,-ap-Rice,* at the *Shefhire-Sheefe,* in *Leek Street.*

A Funeral Sermon
Preached by the Minifter
of Glangothan, in Wales,
probably printed in
London, c. 1750.

SHON-AP-MORGAN, Shentleman of *Wales*, his Journey to *London*

to take Poſſeſſion of his Father's Eſtate. With the Funeral Sermon, preach'd by the Parſon of *Clangothan* in *Wales*, on his Father's Death.

To which is likewiſe annexed,

An *Antient Briton's* Deſcription of his Country, and Character of his Countrymen.

Shon-ap-Morgan,
Shentleman of Wales...,
published by William
Dicey, London, c.1747.

UNNAFRED SHONES, Wife to *Shon-ap-Morgan.*

With her Son and Heir *Morgan-ap-Shones*, going to *London*, to take Possession of the Effects which her late Husband had bequeathed to his dearly beloved Son. With an Inventory of the Goods she left in *Wales*; and the Manner of her taking Leave of her Friends and Relations. *Numb.* 202.

Unnafred Shones, Wife to Shon-ap-Morgan..., published by William Dicey, London, c. 1747.

Datceiniad Penpasdwn,
by Moses Griffith, c.1778.

The Flintshire Whirlegig,
drawn by Francis Grose
after Thomas Pennant,
c.1784.

*Enchantments lately seen
upon the Mountains of
Wales...,* by James Gillray,
published by Hannah
Humphrey, London,
1796.

THE CHURCH MILITANT.

Hear me O Lord for I am poor & needy.

Court Jolly Bacchus Godof Wine

Dying in all it's Branches.
The worst Reds dyed Black:
or any Colour be it ever so bad;
Enquire at the Key and Crook, in
St As--h,
& at the three Cats-Heads in
He--ford.

Kings
Bench

Dernier resort

Trusler's
Sermons

The Reverend captain Pennyless & many others
half dyed and left unfinish'd 178

With spear & scarlet I'm now deck'd,
And sing a jolly song;
But pennyless I must be wreck'd,
On Limbo's rocks eer long.

But hope I spy from Bishops kind,
Like Lighthouse placed high;
If for to change, I heart can find,
Catches in Psalmody.

My scarlet coat I then will doff,
For qeue a grizzle wear;
The outward man I will put off,
And prim as Bawd appear.

Away let Oxford curates trudge,
And starve with learning great:
For Bishops ne'er can wrongly judge,
Who've palm'd my empty pate.
I. Sternhold.

The Church Militant, first
version, after Thomas
Pennant, 1783.

*A Welsh Tandem, by
James Gillray, published
by Hannah Humphrey,
London, 1801.*

The Welsh Curate,
published by Bowles and
Carver, London, c. 1770.

*On a Journey to a
Courtship in Wales,* by
Richard Newton,
published by Holland,
1795.

Monstrosities of 1799,— Scene, Kensington Gardens, by James Gillray, London, 1799.

The Landing of His Majesty, George the Fourth at Holyhead, August 7th, 1821, by Hugh Hughes, 1821.

Taffy's Honor at Stake..., published by Fores, London, 1821.

Y Tories yn cael eu
cymeryd adref at eu teulu,
by James Cope, c. 1834-6

entitled *The Church Militant*. All have the same image of "The Reverend Captain Pennyless" or "Captain Squander", dressed half as a soldier and half as a priest—that is, "half dyed and left unfinish'd". The reference is to the taking of orders and the granting of livings to former army officers returning from the American War of Independence, at the alleged expense of properly trained clergy—the unemployed "Oxford curates". The fate of these unfortunates is given in Sternhold's verses inscribed underneath:

> Away let Oxford Curates trudge,
> And starve with learning great;
> For Bishops ne'er can wrongly judge,
> Who've palm'd my empty pate.[8]

Captain Squander stands destitute outside the King's Bench prison, from which destination he is rescued by taking orders—the "dernier resort". His worldly half says "Come jolly Bacchus, God of wine!" while his spiritual half says "Hear me O Lord for I am poor and needy". Since he knows nothing of theology he relies on the sermons of Dr Trusler who made himself notorious in some quarters in the period by publishing texts in engraved script, resembling handwriting, suitable for the use of untrained or idle clergy. Dean Shipley's father is Pennant's target in this cartoon, along with the Bishop of Hereford, who are both accused of encouraging the abuse:

"Dying in all its branches. The worst Reds (that is, soldiers) dyed Black (that is, made priests): or any colour be it ever so bad; Enquire at the Key and Crook in St. As..h, & at the three Cats-Heads in He..ford."

On the second version of *The Church Militant*, the allusion to these two was obliterated and replaced by a reference to Pennant's comments on the subject in his *Literary Life*. The book was published in 1793, by which time Jonathan Shipley, the absentee Bishop of Saint Asaph, was dead five

The Cries of the Curates or the Growing Evil, after Thomas Pennant, 1783.

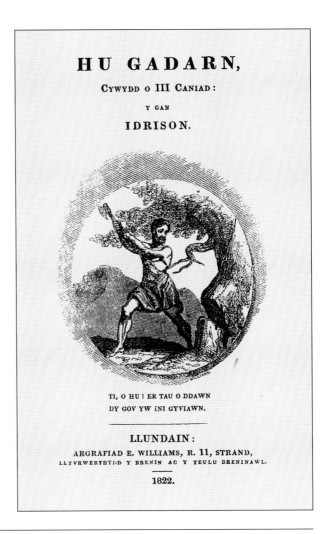

Hu Gadarn, engraved by Abraham Raimbach after William Owen Pughe, 1801.

Owain Jones, Myfyr, engraved by Gauci after John Vaughan, 1828.

Ti, O Hu!..., engraved by Williams after William Owen Pughe, published with his poem *Hu Gadarn*, London, 1822.

years. Pennant probably reissued the print in order to elucidate his comments in the book:

"I am a sincere well-wisher to the pure form of worship of the Church of England, and am highly scandalized if I see any thing wrong in the conduct of our hierarchy. Now and then complaint has been made against the unguarded admission of persons of the most discordant professions into sacred pale, who, urged by no other call than that of poverty, do not prove either ornamental or useful in their new character. To check the progress of a practice injurious to the church, and highly so to those who had spent their fortune in a course of education for the due discharge of their duties, I sent a sarcastic, but salutary print, into the world at which even bishops themselves have deigned to smile."

Pennant's evidence for his last remark was presumably a letter to a newspaper signed by one Laicus:

"Sir, In my walks around this great city, the variety of Prints exhibited at the windows of the shops are no small amusement to me... I speak this because I have lately observed a print which I am sorry to say is as replete with wit as it is with licentiousness, it regards an order of men which I respect as an order notwithstanding the relaxed conduct of Individuals daily lessens what is due to it, the Print I allude to is styled the Church Militant..."

The correspondent, perhaps the Bishop of Chester, goes on to comment on the abuse and to point out its implications in a way with which Pennant would surely have agreed:

"What an occasion does it not give to Methodists and the long list of Schismatics to scoff at our purified religion; how many daily drop away from our flock and either join the enthusiastic tribe or fatally fall into that pit to which Infidelity is sure to lead..."

The Pleasures of the Rail-Road. ___ Cought in the Railway !

Thomas Pennant died in 1798 and with him any substantial Welsh input into English satirical imagery. Despite the presence of a number of artists in London Welsh circles in the late eighteenth century, they do not seem to have interested themselves in political or social satire, nor in the potential of the print for projecting an image of Wales to the world beyond that of the landscape. The societies themselves, given the stimulating visual environment in which they flourished, might have been expected to be active in the promotion of the national image both for the English and for the Welsh audience. With the notable exception of de Loutherbourg's *Last Bard*, which, as we have seen, was published with the work of Edward Jones, Bardd y Brenin, a prominent figure in these circles, they were generally somnolent until the energetic William Owen Pughe awakened them towards the end of the century. Among Pughe's more obsessive fantasies was the figure of Hu Gadarn, a sort of god incarnate who had led the Welsh to Britain from their ancestral home in Sri Lanka. Despite the cynicism of those around him, he persuaded Owain Myfyr to pay for Abraham Raimbach to produce a portrait of his hero to his own design. The only satire associated with this image was in the remarks it drew from Pughe's colleagues. To Jac Glanygors, Hu was "a Welsh Don Quixote", and Dafydd Ddu Eryri asked:

"Does the picture of Hu Gadarn accord with the rules of natural taste and good judgement? Was it a little coracle or a brewer's vat that brought Hu from the land of summer to the Island of Britain?"

Nevertheless, the image of "the old boy jumping out of his coracle with a plough in one hand and a club in the other," as Glanygors put it, persisted long enough to go through various transformations, reproduced both on the medal of the Gwyneddigion Society and as a print. In 1822 a woodcut version of the hero in the process of chopping down a large oak tree decorated the title page of Pughe's poem on the subject, the main virtue of which is its length. In 1831 the same block did service on the title page of *Y Cymro* (The Welshman), a periodical with which Hugh Hughes was closely associated, as we shall see.

Pughe was also involved in a later attempt by the Gwyneddigion to produce prints of more credible national heroes, beginning in 1828 with the engraving by Gauci of a portrait of Owain Myfyr. The original was the work of John Vaughan, but despite the celebrity of the engraver, the results were not to Pughe's satisfaction, giving him occasion for some caustic remarks. Having obtained a copy of the print in Wales, he immediately wrote to the Society, observing that "it is as much like him as it is of the grand Sultan... In the name of goodness was there not one to superintend the copper scratcher to prevent his going on with it?"[9] Undaunted, the Gwyneddigion commissioned Gauci again in 1830, this time to engrave Twm o'r Nant.

By 1824, William Owen Pughe had met Hugh Hughes, and from 1826 they became good friends. As we have seen, Hugh Hughes was earning a living mainly as a wood engraver in London, but it may be that he also engraved social and political satires on copper and stone, although the evidence for this is entirely circumstantial. Between 1828 and 1832, with a few isolated examples in 1833 and 1834, some political cartoons and social satires were published with the signature H.H., in various forms. These have been traditionally ascribed to Henry Heath, a shadowy figure, supposedly a brother to the cartoonist William Heath. Almost nothing is known of him, except that he is believed to have emigrated to Australia. However, two cartoons carrying the H.H. signature and the joint title *The Pleasures of the Rail Road*, were attributed to Hugh Hughes by the connoisseur of prints of technology and industry, Sir Arthur Elton. At the time of this attribution, Hughes was a virtually unknown wood engraver, whereas Henry Heath had a substantial body of caricature associated with his name. Elton, therefore, must have had a particular reason for what would otherwise have been a quite eccentric attribution. Unfortunately, he left no record of his sources. In addition to Elton's attribution, the circumstantial evidence for Hughes as maker of the H.H. prints is three-fold. Firstly, he was politicised and working as an engraver in London at precisely the time in which the prints were published, that is, between 1828 and 1832. The few isolated examples of 1833 and 1834 can easily be accounted for by his subsequent visits to London from Wales. Secondly, he could engrave on copper from early in his career and he later produced lithographs and caricature drawings. Thirdly, the signatures HH and H.H. were both used on wood engravings which are undoubtedly his work.

Hugh Hughes's response to the opposition within his own denomination, the Calvinistic Methodists, to the attempts to remove civil constraints on Catholics in 1828, was to raise a petition in support of the Emancipation Bill from among his own congregation at Jewin Crescent. The consequence was his excommunication at the insistence of the most influential Methodist leader, John Elias. Hughes published a pamphlet on

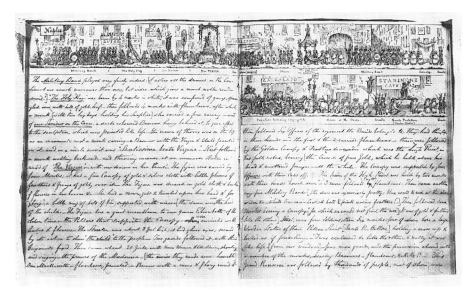

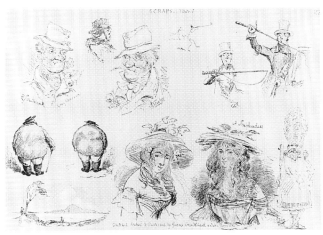

the matter, *Y Trefnyddion a'r Pabyddion* (The Methodists and the Papists), which brought him considerable notoriety as a result of the personal nature of its attack on Elias. Despite being couched in the terms of the late eighteenth-century English satires, as was much of his later writing, it was not accompanied by caricature. Hughes's visual complement to his attack was a straightforward celebration of the leaders of the emancipation movement, Lord Russell and Lord Holland. He produced a mezzotint of his own double portrait inscribed "To the Friends of Religious Freedom".

The only member of the London Welsh circle to display a particular interest in caricature, if Hugh Hughes was not, indeed, responsible for the H.H. cartoons, was John Orlando Parry. Like his father, John Parry, Bardd Alaw, he was a musician. The younger Parry sang and played harp, piano and flageolette. The two were renowned for the duets they played at gatherings of the Gwyneddigion in the late 1820s. However, John Orlando was also an able draughtsman and a painter. He had been born in London and although he visited Wales often, drawing in his diaries and painting landscape, he remained essentially metropolitan, feeding off the energy of the popular culture. He made his career as a music hall entertainer, and this populist inclination also manifested itself in his drawing. In 1833 he visited Paris before travelling on to Italy where he stayed some time, frequenting galleries and theatres. He wrote down his vivid impressions in a series of diaries accompanied by energetic drawings of the people he met and the places he visited. In London he knew George Cruikshank, the foremost political cartoonist of the Regency, well enough to produce caricature drawings with him under the title *Scraps*.[10] These drawings carry the inscription "Sketched and published by George Cruikshank and John Parry Junior", but no printed versions have come to light. Similarly, John Orlando certainly intended his drawing *The Blind Welsh Harper* for publication, since it was highly finished, including the caption. Why he de did not publish the print, having proceeded so far with it, is a mystery.

The Procession of the Virgin, page from the Italian journal of John Orlando Parry, 1834.

Scraps— caricatures by George Cruikshank and John Orlando Parry, c.1835.

CAN YNGHYLCH

SEREN

GYNFFONNOG

...raphwyd yng Nghaerfyrddin gan EVAN POWEL
...homas Roberts. yn y Flwyddyn. 1757

Martial to himselfe / translated

of worldly blessednes, in Latin, English and Walch.

Ex M. valer. Martialis.
ad seipsum. Libro. 10.

Vitam quæ faciant beatiorem
Iocundissi, Martialis hæc sunt,
Res non parta labore, sed relicta,
Non ingratus ager, focus perennis
Lis nunquam, toga rara, mens quieta,
Vires ingenuæ, Salubre corpus,
Prudens simplicitas, pares amici,
Conuictus facilis, sine arte mensa,
Nox non ebria, sed soluta curis,
Non tristis Thorus, attamen pudicus,
Somnus qui faciat breues tenebras,
Quod sis esse velis, nihilq; malis,
Summum nec metuas diem, nec optes.

The same in English.

O Martial, those most merry maite,
These things do make mans life most blest,
Goods not gotten by labour great,
But left by friendes, new gaus to rest,
A fruitfull fielde, a fyre styll hoote,
Fay suer by strife no tymes to striue,
A sobouse gowne, a quiet minde.

Strength naturall, a body sound,
We pure simplenes, frienaes like to thee,
Al cousions easy to be found,
A table where no Caterers be,
No drunken night, but from cares frie,
No doisfull bed, yet of chast taste,
Sleape that may make the darknes short.

That thing that thou thy selfe art minde,
And by wish lot pourtat to ber,
And thou thy selfe firmly perswade,
Stull to remayne in selfe degree,
And let nought be more waight of this,
The day of death feare not ame what,
Nay yet to thou wish after it.

The same in the Britishe
tong. which the people at this
day in the English Barons
spreche, call Walche.

Traethawt Martial vardd
am wynwyd new dded wryddit by dol.

Gant yi ordd gnot ar abbyst,
Gwe baeth yn agoli byst.
Gawi bort eb bn cymat bryth
Marcial ordd bwnw inotwyfyth.
Diddan bydol dedtwyddyd.
Dwys gosa noaes yayd,
Dne byn mewn teiurbi call
Deubeth ar bematebr dibyll

1 Helaeth ddarawtwyniol sive.
Hen ei gael byny brafael byni
2 Traba daw: tir ddhwtat,
Cann yd trow yn tar
3 Can tymboraidd ar wynny
Tec auultre marwn ddewe dy,
4 Illae e bra digtiawn bnin
Y digwhias Gyfraith byaddin:
5 Inwynych gynefinate
I fwydd a bair dyawngturdd ayaie,
6 Da beddtwl gwyw deithwl gian,
Digyn wyf deeddhg arian.
7 Egul corph that annoe hatwl.
Aru gaiu, byde yn gwn drdyatcl,
8 Coel eb antwir. carl beuarbd.
Corph tach i ddtwyn cytwt fydd,
9 Cotns' wirtaubet cyhawn.
Call btwys, ni phair coiti datwn:
10 Cyuderthion gietwten gian,
Crydydd. du dddidiart erbuen,
11 Iach hoff gyfr dbach e chair
Dotnnynad dda n biatt,
12 Glan byydd byb ar hugiatwn baerh
Gynnal mantwl gaginiartb,
13 Nos dro iai nak a deitrth
Difedda (pant da bydd y petb)
14 Drwis hoff wely ddwair,
Didylld buod dlt yb ft a baeg,
15 Hun a dwerlo norb bitwg,
Deallee brybywri'trg.
16 Aa wylilwilo n twerli iiod,
Aoc bydd. yn bine ei bod.
17 Yrbotrn bu nees efnbau
Y bywedddat oi byddiau.
TERVYN.

Simon Vachan ei cycanuwdd wrth
arch ac esponiat M. S. Ih.
1571.

Imprinted at London by
John Awdely.

V The woodcut revival and the broadsheet ballad

In 1757, in Priory Street, Carmarthen, Evan Powell printed a moralising ballad on the ancient theme of a comet, *Can Ynghylch Seren Gynffonog*. He illustrated the title page with a rough but energetic woodcut. The image of the comet was remembered by Evan Powell from English ballads on which it had appeared for a hundred years and more, but the block was almost certainly cut especially for the publication, presumably by the printer himself. Welsh-language texts of various sorts, including ballads, had been illustrated occasionally with woodcuts for many years, but Evan Powell's effort was certainly among the first illustrations made in Wales itself. The image was an appropriate one. With the exception of an isolated effort in the sixteenth century, printing made a late start in Wales, held back by the Licensing Act. However, once established, it would grow with the rapidity of Powell's approaching comet to become not only a productive industry but also a central pillar of Welsh consciousness and, for radicals, a symbol of national progress.

Until the change in the law, almost all Welsh-language texts had been printed in London. Some had been illustrated beyond the inclusion of conventional decorations. Among the most remarkable was Simwnt Fychan's translation of Martial's *Epigram on the Happy Life*, done in 1571. It has a mysterious woodcut, presumably designed by the translator himself, of three interlocked crescent moons and Hebrew words, reflecting the astrological and cabalistic interests of the period.[1] However, its erudite references and the intellectual pedigree of Simwnt Fychan, who inherited through his teacher, Gruffydd Hiraethog, the traditions of the professional bardic order, hardly qualify it as popular art. Nearer the mark is a broadside of 1591 in the form of a brief granted to Sion Salisburi of Gwyddelwern, illustrated with very appropriate woodcuts of a ship, Queen Elizabeth, and a coat of arms.

A number of emigré Welsh people in sixteenth-century London were involved in printing, publishing and bookselling, the trade collectively known as "stationer". One of them, Richard Jones, certainly interested himself in the popular end of the market, printing ballads and broadsides. The Stationer's Register for 20 March 1587 gives the following entries under his name:

"Receaved of him for pryntinge of *a Sonett or a synners Solace* made by HUGHE GRYFFYTHE prysoner, bothe in Welche and Englishe, iiijd.

"Receaved of him for pryntinge an *Epitaphe of the Death of Sir* YEVAN LLOYD *of Yale knighte* made by the said Hughe Gryffithe, iiijd".[2]

Despite the appellation "popular", the circulation of such material was presumably very small, extending little beyond Welsh speakers in London, and—in this case, perhaps—the interested inhabitants of Wrexham. As far as is known, no means of distributing such material existed in Wales at the time, beyond passing from hand to hand odd copies bought by travellers in London. Not until after the Commonwealth, when Thomas Jones yr Almanaciwr began his work, was any serious attempt made to develop the market. After the revision of the Licensing Act, Thomas Jones moved his operations from London to Shrewsbury, a much more convenient centre for the distribution of Welsh-language material. In his collection *Llyfr Carolau a Dyriau Duwiol* (A Book of Carols and Godly Poems) of 1696, and in his almanacks, he included poems written by Siôn Rhydderch of Cemmaes. Two years after the death of Thomas Jones, in 1713, Siôn Rhydderch was himself printing in Shrewsbury. Where he learnt the trade is unknown, but it could well have been at the side of his former publisher, especially since his earliest known product was an almanack. In 1716 he published *Gweledigaeth Dafydd Evans* (The Vision of Dafydd Evans), a poem of seventy verses, and the oldest surviving example of his work to carry a woodcut on the title page. It is a formal decoration, no doubt bought in by the printer, but by the following year he had either cut for himself or commissioned a special block, an early example of the corporate image. He used this logo—"JR" for John Rhydderch, the Anglicised version of his name—regularly as his imprint.

Can Ynghylch Seren Gynffonog, by Evan Powell, Carmarthen, 1757.

Martial to himselfe/treating of wordly blessednes, in Latin, English and Walsch, translated by Simwnt Fychan, London, 1571.

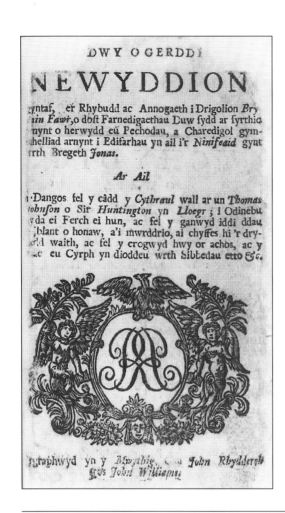

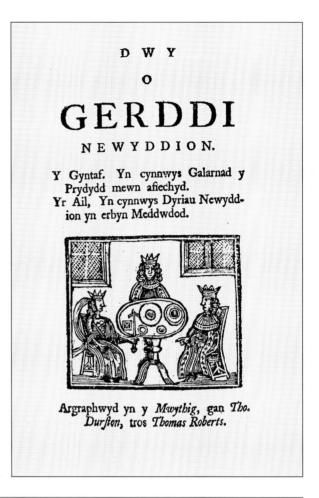

Dwy o Gerddi Newyddion..., printed by Siôn Rhydderch for John Williams, Shrewsbury, c.1717-29.

Dwy o Gerddi Newyddion, printed by Thomas Durston for Thomas Roberts, Shrewsbury, c.1730.

Eighteenth-century ballads were infrequently illustrated—less than fifty examples have survived—but this had little to do with a particular lack of interest on the part of Welsh producers. The medium was also in decline in England when Welsh material began to be produced in quantity. Although old blocks were copied, the main creative energy was being expended in the field of the intaglio prints, as we have seen.

Siôn Rhydderch's career as a printer in Shrewsbury came to an abrupt end in 1729 when he had to sell all his equipment as the result of domestic troubles, the nature of which are not entirely clear. The affair seems to have involved an English printer of the town, Thomas Durston, who certainly took full advantage of the absence of Siôn Rhydderch to develop the Welsh-language market. Durston sometimes copied Siôn Rhydderch's texts but was more adventurous with pictures. His edition of two ballads by Ellis Rowland and Morgan Lloyd, done for Thomas Roberts, is identical to Siôn Rhydderch's original version printed in 1728, except that it has a good woodcut on the title page. In Chester, Elizabeth Adams and T. Huxley offered their Welsh customers illustrations to make their products more saleable, into the 1760s.

The simplicity of the few blocks used by printers in Wales in the mid-eighteenth century suggests strongly that they were cut on the premises, rather than bought in from England. John Rowland, for instance, who set up his press in Bala in 1761, used a number of blocks alongside ballads by Ellis y Cowper and others.

Having been ousted from Shrewsbury, Siôn Rhydderch appealed to Lewis Morris for help in his distress. Their discussions seem to have led to the far-sighted but ill-fated proposal of Lewis Morris to establish a press at Llannerchymedd by public subscription in 1731. A press was bought and Siôn Rhydderch was certainly intended to be the printer, but lack of public support prevented the further development of the project. The only product of the press was the first Welsh-language periodical, *Tlysau yr Hen Oesoedd* (The Treasures of Olden Times), printed in 1735 though not by Siôn Rhydderch. The printer had left for Carmarthen, which would develop

Two Ballads, printed by Ismael Davies, Trefriw, c.1785-1810.

as the main centre of publishing in Wales by the end of the century.

Nevertheless, Lewis Morris's press would eventually do important work. According to a story which acquired folk-lore status among the Welsh literati in the later nineteenth century, the press was bought and set up in 1776 at Trefriw by Dafydd Jones, the first of four generations of printers in the family. Dafydd Jones apparently had no inclination to illustrate his work, but his son, Ishmael Davies, was somewhat more adventurous. In his time the press had about half a dozen rather tentative but pretty illustrations, probably cut locally. However, under the direction of his son, John Jones, the press changed its attitude to illustration dramatically, and turned out the best and most original work done in the medium in Wales. By the mid-1830s, the Venedotian Press was producing ballads with pictures to small and large formats in considerable numbers, as well as illustrated books and periodicals.

The interest of John Jones in illustration was certainly due in some measure to the activities of Hugh Hughes, who brought with him from London first-hand knowledge of the revival of the woodcut in the English popular press at the start of the nineteenth century. The revival had been facilitated by the artistic success of Thomas Bewick and the entrepreneurial acumen of a number of writers and publishers in expanding the range of material offered on the mass market. Bewick cut his images on the end grain of the wood block rather than along the grain, enabling him to achieve much finer detail and a wider range of effects. The technique is called wood engraving as distinct from the woodcut, and although Bewick was not the first to use it, his brilliant technique, applied to the illustration of

a number of prestigious volumes, brought it into high fashion in the English art world. Nevertheless, the influence of the finer quality of the wood engraving made itself felt on a much wider range of material than expensive volumes such as his *General History of Quadrupeds*, published in 1790. Bewick drew his own originals even though he had been trained as an artisan rather than in an art academy, and he applied his brilliant technique to advertisements, tickets and business cards as readily as he did to expensive books. He worked in Newcastle, where there was a long-standing tradition of popular woodcuts, and though he himself disliked London intensely, he trained a generation of engravers who moved south.

Along with many of his apprentices, the son of Bewick's Newcastle printer also moved to London. From 1813, James Catnach entered into competition with John Pitts, established since 1802, and between them they revitalised the woodcut as a visual medium in the popular press.[3] In particular, both publishers developed the large format ballad and broadside, in which the pictures were the dominant element, reviving the tradition of the single sheets, such as *Shon-ap-Morgan, Shentilman of Wales*, produced by the chapbook publishers nearly a century before. Catnach was able to print in very large numbers. He is known to have put out 500,000 copies of *The Murder of William Weare* in eight days. The potential market for popular literature in England was beginning to be exploited through a wide variety of material on a mass scale. For instance, the "Cheap Repository Tracts" of Hannah More sold two million copies in 1795, laying the foundations of the Religious Tract Society, set up four years later. The moralising tone of the tracts was not dissimilar in sentiment to many of the ballads issued by Pitts and Catnach, despite the difference of style. They were complementary to each other in the encouragement of the habit of reading, and probably shared a large part of the audience.

| 1 | 2 | 3 | 4 |

DO,

RE,

MI,

FA,

| Gosoder blaen y tafod o dan y dannedd uchaf, ond heb fod rhwng y dannedd. | Ysgydwed neu darawed y tafod rhwng y dannedd. | Tarawed y gwefusau yn ynghyd. | Tarawed y dannedd uchaf ar y wefus isaf. |

It was exactly in this period of expansion, beginning in 1804 when he was apprenticed as an engraver, that Hugh Hughes was in close contact with the influence both of Bewick and of Catnach. Hughes probably worked for the wood engraver William Hughes, a pupil of Henry Hole who had, in turn, been a pupil of Bewick. His collection of wood engravings, *The Beauties of Cambria*, brought him to prominence amongst Welsh intellectuals. It was an avant-garde production since the technique had not previously been used to illustrate a description of landscape, and was aimed at the upper end of the market—it was priced at two guineas. Nevertheless, it seems certain that in the same period, from 1814 until 1832, Hughes was also producing blocks for the popular press in London. In 1828 he moved to live in Greek Street, only a stone's throw from Seven Dials, the disreputable area made famous by John Gay in *The Beggar's Opera*, which was the home of Catnach's business. Catnach's engravers rarely signed their works, and attribution is difficult since the conventions of the medium caused many of them to work in a very similar way. Nevertheless, there are especially striking similarities of style and technique between some prints published on Catnach's large illustrated ballads and popular prints for Welsh publishers known to be by Hughes. Among these are his four illustrations for *Yr Hynafion Cymreig* (The Welsh Antiquities), published in 1823 by John Evans in Carmarthen.

Hugh Hughes had a mission for the spiritual and practical progress of the people, to be accomplished by reading in the Welsh language. As we have seen, he often used the image of reading or writing in his wood engravings. He was inspired by the use of the picture in the English popular press as a means of making reading matter more attractive. As well as being themselves a new departure, his engravings illustrated texts that pioneered new fields in the Welsh language, such as children's literature and textbooks on music. In 1816 his portrait of John Ellis adorned *Mawl i'r Arglwydd* (Praise to the Lord), and two years later he provided the curious pictures in Owen Williams's *Egwyddorion Canu* (The Principles of Singing). Almost all of the original illustrations published in Welsh-language texts for the next fourteen years were his work. He travelled extensively in Wales, working with John Evans in Carmarthen, Thomas Gee in Denbigh, John Cox in Aberystwyth, and Robert Saunderson in Bala. Most appropriately, his work for Saunderson was to produce illustrations for the covers of Welsh-language versions of Legh Richmond's stories published by the Religious Tract Society, including *Merch y Llaethwr* (The Dairyman's Daughter) and *Hanes Jane Fach* (The Young Cottager). He provided most of the illustrations for the first two periodicals regularly to use pictures. His work for John Evans's *Seren Gomer* (Star of Gomer) included a series of six animals though the quality of the blocks was spoiled by the poor paper used in the magazine. Hughes was involved in London with *Y Cymro* as an editor as well as

Cyfarwyddyd i Ffurfio y genau...., by Hugh Hughes, from Egwyddorion Canu by Owen Williams, 1818.

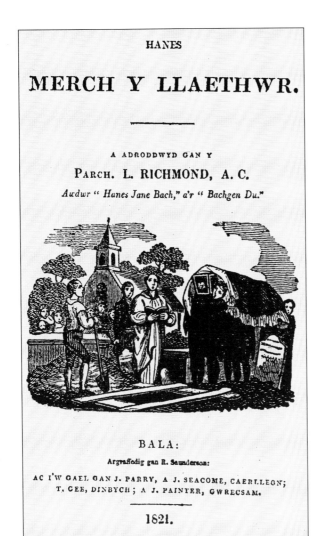

HANES

MERCH Y LLAETHWR.

A ADRODDWYD GAN Y

PARCH. L. RICHMOND, A. C.

Audwr " Hanes Jane Bach," a'r " Bachgen Du."

BALA:

Argraffedig gan R. Saunderson:

AC I'W GAEL GAN J. PARRY, A J. SEACOME, CAERLLEON;
T. GEE, DINBYCH; A J. PAINTER, GWRECSAM.

1821.

Mae gorthrymderau lawer yn y byd,
Aflendid, poen, a blinder, &c.
Galaethus hudoliaethau,
Mawr ystryw, llu o rwystrau
Gyfodir, a gofidiau, &c.
Ac aml a blin gystuddiau, &c.

Nid oes dim gorthrymderau yn y Nef,
Euogrwydd blin, na phoenau, &c.
Mae pawb yn berffaith ddedwydd,
Oll yno, mewn llawenydd,
A heddwch pûr na dderfydd, &c.
Heb rwystrau, poen, na chystudd, &c.

The Funeral, by Hugh Hughes, cover for *Hanes Merch y Llaethwr* by Legh Richmond, published by Robert Saunderson, Y Bala, 1821.

Y Cawrfil, by Hugh Hughes, from *Seren Gomer,* published by John Evans, Carmarthen, 1829.

illustrator and the quality of the prints was much better. Although of little visual interest, his technical diagrams illustrating scientific writing by Griffith Davies were, again, a pioneering venture in the Welsh language. However, his closest association was with John Jones of Llanrwst, and although Hughes gave up wood engraving in 1832 because of the deterioration of his eyesight, it cannot be coincidental that it is at about that time that John Jones ventured into printing large format ballad sheets in which the illustrations are the dominant element.[4]

Some of John Jones's prints brought images known throughout Europe for hundreds of years into Welsh-language culture for the first time. His versions of the Stages of Life theme were transmitted through Catnach's English interpretations. John Jones owned a set of the nine basic blocks of the ageing couple, and versions of "Infancy" and "100 Years Old", which—as on the Catnach version—were to a different format. He accompanied his blocks on *Deuddeg Tymor Bywyd* (The Twelve Ages of Man) with verses which were free adaptions from the English prints. *Myfyrdod ar Ddyn* (A Meditation on Mankind), a different edition, had original but still anonymous verses. In the 1830s, the casting of metal copies of original woodcuts became common. The process was known as stereotyping, the original meaning of a word which came to be used in a much wider sense. However, since John Jones's collection of wood blocks has survived, we know that he had only a very few stereotypes. Like the verses which accompanied *Deuddeg Tymor Bywyd*, the blocks were free interpretations of the English versions, not precise copies. Many of Jones's blocks, including the Stages of Life, may have been cut by Hugh Hughes, but it is impossible to say for certain.

Among John Jones's best small blocks were a set of tradespeople and shopkeepers, of whom a number seem to be in serious contention with their customers. The printer used them frequently, both as singles on

small format ballads and on periodicals such as *Yr Athraw i Blentyn*. They also appear as fillers on large sheets. On *Y Byd Helbulus a'r Nefoedd Hapus* (The Troubled World and the Happy Heaven) they were put to more appropriate use than usual, representing the contentions of this world, divided by a strong horizontal line from two angels and Christ at the Last Supper, representing the peace of Heaven. They accurately reflect the anonymous verses, a shopping list of woes demonstrating the sophistication of the language of misery achieved after a hundred years of refinement by puritan poets:

> There's great oppression in this world,
> Corruption, pain and toil, &.
> And woeful the deception,
> Great trickery and frustration,
> That rise for our affliction
> And grievous tribulation, &.
>
> There's no oppression high in Heaven
> Nor grievous guilt nor pain, &.
> Each rests in perfect happiness,
> Eternal joy and bliss,
> All in unending peace they live, &.
> No pain, frustration, grief, &.

Although the source of the small blocks is difficult to determine, one of the two angels on this print carries the signature of James Cope. John Jones owned a dozen signed blocks by Cope and there are a further twenty that can be confidently attributed to him on the grounds of their distinctive style. James Cope was born somewhere in Caernarfonshire in 1805 or 1806, married Jane in about 1825, and by 1841 had three children, Sarah, 15, Jane, 13, and Elizabeth, 10. They lived in Chapel Street in Caernarfon.

Y Byd Helbulus a'r Nefoedd Hapus, including blocks by James Cope, c.1832-42, published by John Jones, Llanrwst.

93

Ni ddianc gradd nac oedran,
tra buan yw ei dro,
Na'r ifangc hardd na'r henddyn,
na'r plentyn aned ddoe.

Merthyrdod y Saint a'r Apostolion, including a block by James Cope, c.1832-42, published by John Jones, Llanrwst.

Bywyd a Dyoddefaint Crist, block by James Cope, c.1832-42, published by John Jones, Llanrwst.

He produced political cartoons which were anti-Tory and anti-Church, suggesting that he was a radical Nonconformist. It seems likely that all the surviving blocks were made in the decade before 1842. Beyond these few facts and speculations, little more can be said, except that with the remarkable woodcuts of James Cope, printed pictures in the popular press finally blossomed in Wales.

On John Jones's large format sheet *Merthyrdod y Saint a'r Apostolion* (The Martyrdom of the Saints and Apostles), James Cope's image of the risen Christ, the crown of thorns lifted from his head and in his hand an orb, symbolising his care for the world, is flanked by twelve early Christian martyrs and the four evangelists. The text briefly explains the manner of death of the martyrs as a prelude to the ballad *Hanes Pechod, yr hwn yw Colyn Angau* (The Story of Sin, that is the Sting of Death). Though it is not attributed to him here, the ballad had been written by Dafydd William, a Methodist turned Baptist hymn writer. Like many others of its genre, it is a sort of potted version of the Bible, leaving out the boring bits, with a strong emphasis on human wickedness and its likely consequences:

> None will escape, soon to be judged,
>   not the mighty nor the old,
> Not the young and fair, the aged and worn,
>   nor the new-born, still and cold.

The image of Christ has different stylistic characteristics to those of the saints and evangelists. The Christ, like the unidentified circular image which accompanies a ballad by Ywain Meirion and a translation of an American hymn by David Charles, under the title *Bywyd a dyoddefaint Crist* (The Life and Suffering of Christ), is derived from intaglio engravings of high-art originals probably transmitted through London prints where it is common. It is in a wood engraving style, if not, in fact, cut on the end

94

grain. The use of a realistic landscape background and tint—the close parallel lines cut with a comb-like tool to give greater density and atmosphere—contrast with the medieval simplicity of the saints which are closer to seventeenth-century woodcuts. James Cope certainly worked in both ways, and it is possible that all these blocks are by him. He had a love of fanciful, exotic and supernatural imagery with which the bizarre interpretation of the eagle with Saint Matthew and the angel with Saint Mark are consistent. The iconography and identification of the saints in the captions has been muddled, suggesting a decayed tradition with which the publisher was not thoroughly familiar. For John Jones, it seems, a saint was a saint.

Jones made frequent use of these blocks of the martyrs and evangelists, a fact which suggests they were popular with the public. They occur on various versions of his print *Myfyrdod ar y Cloc yn Taro* (A Meditation on the Striking Clock). The ballad expresses an appropriate sentiment for each hour struck in the form of a correspondence between the number and a biblical event or characters, to which a precise reference is given—a Christian gloss on the ancient fascination of the people with mystical numbers and astrology, maintained in the almanacks. The ballad is rather more optimistic in tone than Dafydd William's doom-laden *Colyn Angau*, which may account for its popularity:

In depth of meditation,
The bell chimed one o'clock,
I saw that I must worship
One God, he is my rock;
And also I must serve him,
My heart with gladness fill,
While on this earth I'm waiting
And life continues, still...

Myfyrdod ar y Cloc yn Taro, published by John Jones, Llanrwst, c. 1830-60.

ELIAS

YN CAEL EI BORTHI GAN Y CIGFRAIN.

"A'r cigfrain a ddygent iddo fara a chig y bore, a bara a chig brydnawn:
ac efe a yfai o'r afon."—1 Bren. xvii., 6.

*Elias yn cael ei borthi gan
y Cigfran,* block by James
Cope, c.1832-42,
published by O.E. Jones,
Llanrwst, c.1865.

But soon she called out midnight,
The circle come full round,
My body lying under,
For ever in the ground;
My soul to heaven flying,
The world of living ghosts,
Where I shall stay, eternal,
Among the good Lord's hosts.

A few of James Cope's woodcuts are known in what is, in all probability, their original published form. However, from their context or the date of the imprint, it is clear that many others have survived only as they were re-used at a later date. It is apparent, therefore, that the surviving examples of illustrated ballad sheets represent only a proportion—probably a small proportion—of those published. Although the three blocks and the text of *Elias yn cael ei borthi gan y Cigfrain* (Elias Fed by the Crows) belong together, their awkward composition and the imprint of Evan Jones, son of John Jones (which gives a date no earlier than 1865, at least twenty-three years after they were cut), suggest strongly that—separately or apart—they belong originally to a lost sheet.

Two of Cope's surviving large woodcuts, each made from three blocks, may originally have formed part of a series made to a common format. *Abraham yn Aberthu Isaac* (Abraham Sacrificing Isaac), like *Elias...,* is known only from a late version but is coupled with what was probably its original ballad. It depicts the moment of greatest drama when the angel commands Abraham not to kill his son and points to the ram caught in a thicket:

Ei unig Fab a rwymai
A'r gyllell yn ei law,
Ond bloeddiwyd arno Attal,
Dros gaer y nefoedd draw.

A gwelai hwrdd mewn drysni
Yn aberth rhwydd i'w roi
"Offryma hwn yn aberth,
A gad i'r bachgen ffoi".

Abr'ham bound his only son,
A knife held in his hand,
But "stop" a voice called to him
From heaven's ramparts grand.

Behold caught in a thicket,
The ram is yours to give,
Kill him upon the altar
And let the young child live.

Abraham yn aberthu Isaac, block by James Cope, c.1832-42, published by O.E. Jones, Llanrwst, c.1865.

This image was cut in Cope's simpler, woodcut style. His detailing was bold and exotic on many of his blocks, but at its finest here in the patterns on the altar and the clothes of the participants, and in the luxuriant foliage of the background which combines oak leaves and palm trees. He appears to have made a mistake in working on the block, since Abraham's hand has been drilled out and a plug inserted before being re-cut.

Among Cope's most ambitious works was a crucifixion scene which, unfortunately, survives only in part on the sheet *Golwg ar y Groes neu fyfyrdodau ar Groeshoeliad Iesu Grist* (A View of the Cross, or a Meditation on the Crucifixion of Jesus Christ). Only the two right-hand blocks have been printed, supported by small blocks borrowed from other sources. Cope's signature probably appeared on the missing left-hand block. The scene is depicted in sombre tones with heavy tints used to suggest the darkness of the ninth hour. Above Christ's head, instead of INRI is the word MARW—death. The three Maries are at Christ's feet, and Mary, mother of Christ, is also prominent, of course, in Cope's two surviving nativities. The subjects are *The Adoration of the Shepherds*, an unsigned print in the simpler style, and *The Three Wise Men*, signed and cut in the tighter style with a heavy shaded border suggesting a picture frame surrounding a painting. The depiction of Mary on these prints does not

97

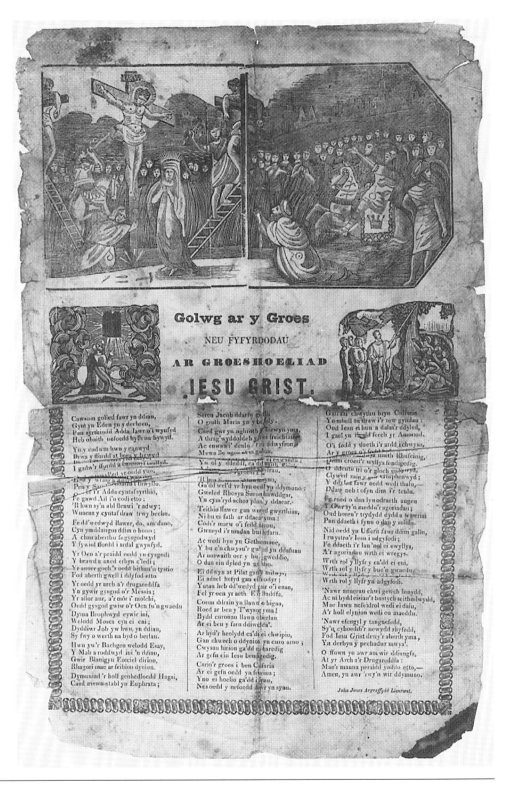

Golwg ar y Groes..., block
by James Cope, c. 1832-
42, published by John
Jones, Llanrwst.

represent anything approaching a cult of the Virgin, and, indeed, no
Madonna and Child by Cope is known. Nevertheless, Cope's religious
subjects undermine the received wisdom about Welsh Nonconformist
attitudes to religious pictures. The common perception of devotion in the
Puritan tradition, cultivated by nineteenth-century writers, is at odds with
the practice of the people. We have seen that preachers themselves
became the subject of an extensive popular iconography in a nation
whose leaders, by the mid-nineteenth century, liked to boast of the purity
of the Protestant faith as a characteristic national virtue. The popularity of
the ballad sheets makes it quite clear that, just as in Catholic France where
biblical scenes were the mainstay of *Imagerie*, so also in Nonconformist
Wales, religious pictures were produced and bought on a large scale.
James Cope was almost certainly a Nonconformist and his printer, John
Jones, worshipped with the Independents after his marriage (although he

had previously been an Anglican). The other large-scale producer of this type of religious imagery, Isaac Thomas of Cardigan, was a Baptist deacon.

Further evidence of the appetite of the people for religious pictures comes from reports of the activities of hawkers of the brilliantly coloured and framed pictures on glass still seen in many houses. Among the most common subjects were the Madonna and Child. To complicate matters further, according to first-hand witnesses, the hawkers were Jewish. The painter Carey Morris from Llandeilo remembered that when he was a child, in about 1890, "it was a familiar sight to see itinerant vendors displaying most gaudy and highly-coloured reproductions of religious pictures to the simple country folk. The vendors were invariably sons of Israel and the pictures were obviously Roman Catholic in sentiment; the subjects were the Madonna and Child and the Crucifixion, very gaudily coloured and the general effect considerably heightened and made more attractive to the people by a liberal supply of gold and silver tinsel decoration. As a boy these pictures and the itinerant visitors fascinated me. Some years later it struck me a most remarkable sight—Jewish vendors selling Roman Catholic pictures to Nonconformists." Carey Morris's recollection is confirmed by W.H. Davies who mentioned that he "had framed many a print for Jew hawkers to take into the Welsh hills."[5]

The imagery of James Cope derived from pre-Protestant traditions of Medieval and Renaissance painting, sculpture and glass, extending throughout Europe. The transmission of the iconography to the popular prints was through intaglio prints of high art originals, reinterpreted by generations of designers and engravers, each one producing variants of the same designs. The prints were available from booksellers and from itinerant print sellers like the J. Caple who held a sale of "an immense stock of engravings" at Cardigan in 1839.[6] However, the most important source was certainly the illustrated Bibles of the later eighteenth century of which there were many, such as *Wood's New Family Bible* printed and illustrated at Shrewsbury in 1777. The iconography of Wood's picture of *Christ going to be crucified*, depicted according to Saint Luke, is largely shared by the *Road to Calvary* printed by John Jones as a Christmas carol with a ballad by T. Harris. Christ is given a halo in the popular version.

Carol Nadolig Yn Gosod, Allan Enedigaeth Bywyd a Marwolaeth, Iesu Grist, block probably by James Cope, c.1832-42, published by John Jones, Llanrwst.

Christ going to be crucified, engraved by Rothwell after Mignard, from *Wood's Family Bible*, Shrewsbury, 1777.

The Adoration of the Shepherds by James Cope, c.1832-42, published by John Jones, Llanrwst.

Some of John Jones's religious ballads were accompanied by images translated directly from London popular prints. The Resurrection printed with John James's *Cerdd yn Gosod allan Fraint y rhai a obeithiant yn yr Arglwydd* (A Song Setting forth the Privilege of those who have hope in the Lord) is copied from a Catnach print. This image, like *The Road to Calvary* may be by Cope, though neither is signed and both are more crudely done than most of his work. James Cope's finest biblical picture, *Adda ac Efa yn Ngardd Eden* (Adam and Eve in the Garden of Eden), demonstrates his normal practice of reinterpreting the ancient iconography. The subjects of the Earthly Paradise and the Fall were among the most attractive to the people and appear not only in the popular prints but also in the work of artisan and naive painters and of embroiderers. The numerous versions done by Edward Hicks, the most famous interpreter of the theme, and the prints of James Cope are strikingly similar and demonstrate the wide distribution of the common sources. The two were working at the same time, but Hicks lived in the north-eastern United States. The imagery used by James Williams of Wrexham for the subject of "Adam naming the Animals" on his great embroidery made between 1842 and 1852, also reflects the same sources. He was almost certainly familiar with popular prints such as the *Adda ac Efa* and *Arch Noah*, in which many of the animals were clearly derived from Bewick's *Quadrupeds*. The religious imagery familiar to working people like James Williams was the result of a complex process of cross-fertilisation between high art and popular forms.[7]

Printed with Cope's *Adda ac Efa* was *Yr Hwsmon Diog a'r Cristion Diofal* (The Lazy Farmer and the Careless Christian) by John Thomas of Pentre'r Foelas. Thomas had died in 1818 but his works were not printed together until 1854 in the John Jones edition, edited by William Williams, Caledfryn. The version on the ballad sheet is earlier since it does not include Caledfryn's tidying up of the grammar and punctuation. The ballad begins with the Fall:

> In EDEN's fine garden, life's only true origin,
>   My Father, he ruled there, a lord;
> Turned out to be tortured, his power dishonoured,
>   Because he would break God's accord.

However, the main moralising idea is closer to home—an analogy between a lazy farmer and a careless Christian:

> His heart still corrupted, a man unconverted
>   Like land never tilled, it remains;
> A tree long since planted that bears no fruit on it,
>   To love such a plant we disdain.

ADDA ac EFA
Yn Ngardd Eden.

YR HWSMON DIOG AR CRISTION DIOFAL.

Cenir ar "God save the King," yr hen ffordd.

YN EDEN, fan odiaeth, y bu fy nhrefnadaeth,
A Nhad yno 'n benaeth yn byw ;
Fe'i troed i boenydio yn ddiuerth oddiyno,
Am iddo fo ddigio'r gwir Dduw ;
...

JOHN THOMAS.

JOHN JONES, ARGRAFFYDD, LLANRWST.

Let all of us struggle, through old age and trouble,
    And never presume ourselves grand,
There is in the dark grave no work nor advantage,
    Each hour we must readily stand.

Adda ac Efa Yn Ngardd Eden, block by James Cope, c.1832-42, published by John Jones, Llanrwst.

Funereal imagery was common in the moralising popular literature—even in children's literature. The *Addysgydd* produced by Hugh Hughes and David Charles in 1823, contains the story of a small boy made to ponder on the state of his soul by walking through a churchyard. He carries a stick by means of which he discovers that some of the graves are shorter than the others—children's graves:

"He ran home in haste, and said, 'I too must think about dying; there are

Rhedodd gartref gydâ brys, ac a
ddywedodd, 'Rhaid i finnau feddwl am farw;
y mae beddau yn y fynwent yna yn fyrach
nâ'r un bedd eisiau arnaf *fi* gael'.

Ddarllenydd! y mae yn amser bellach i tithau
feddwl yn sobr. Pwy a wyr na cheir dithau, er
mor ieuanc ydwyt, ac mor iach heddyw, yn
nghanol y meirwon, · dan yr Ywen ddudew
fawr, · yn y fynwent ddystaw, cyn pen
blwyddyn, · cyn pen mis, · cyn pen wythnos...

P'le mae'r dynion doeth llafurus?
P'le mae'r lleill fu'n byw'n esgeulus?
P'le mae'r diwyd? P'le mae'r diogyn?
Oll yn gydradd yn y dyffryn.

Gogoniant fyth fo i enw'r Iesu,
Am ein cadw a'n diogelu:
Dwg ni, o Dduw, i'th nefoedd lawen
Amen, Amen, ni oll dymunem.

Myfyrdod ar farwolaeth...,
block by James Cope,
c.1832-42, published by
John Jones, Llanrwst.

Y Bedd..., block by James
Cope, c.1832-42,
published by John Jones,
Llanrwst.

graves in the churchyard that are shorter than any grave *I* would need.'
"Reader! The time has come for you too to think carefully. Who knows that
you also, although so young and so healthy today, will not find yourself
among the dead,—under the great dark yew,—in the quiet graveyard,
before a year is out,—before a month,—before a week..."

Cope provided at least two visual accompaniments to such sober
warnings published by John Jones. R. Williams's *Myfyrdod ar Farwolaeth*
(Meditation on Death) and an anonymous *Myfyrdod mewn Mynwent*
(Meditation in a Graveyard) both use a large unsigned block in the simpler
style showing an internment in front of a church. The *Myfyrdod mewn
Mynwent* is a particularly depressing composition of 36 substantial doom-
laden verses. R. Williams's meditation has a more jaunty rhythm, further
enlivened by the mysterious inclusion of a small block of an ostrich hunt in

the sky above the grieving party round the grave.

Cope's signed funeral scene, accompanied by the cheery *Y Bedd—"Y Ty Rhagderfynedig i bob dyn byw"* (The Grave—"The Predestined Home of all Men") is a grander affair, depicting the scene in some detail, with the hearse and a coach (repeated above in a silhouette block not by Cope), a long line of mourners and the sexton. The symbolic content is strong with the sun disappearing into the sea and a wind-blown winter tree. The theme, presumably intended to encourage the downtrodden populace, is the equality of the grave:

> Where the wise who laboured, tireless?
> Where the rest who wasted, heedless?
> Where the diligent? Where the lazy?
> All are equal in the valley.

Two of Cope's more optimistic images depict the Christian's hope of victory over death. Though probably not intended originally to accompany it, the final verse of *Genedigaeth, bywyd pur, a diben dyfodiad ein Harglwydd Iesu Grist i'r byd* (The birth, pure life, and purpose of the coming of our Lord Jesus Christ to the world) by Richard Jones of Llanllechyd is an appropriate counterpart to the vision of the gates of Heaven:

> Eternal glory be to Jesus,
> He who guards and keeps and saves us:
> Lord bring us to your joyful heaven!
> Amen, Amen, cry all the risen.

The image may be intended as a resurrection since a tree seems to be pushed aside and a child carried upwards by an angel to the accompani-

Block by James Cope from *Can Newyddd yn gosod allan Enedigaeth, bywyd pur, a diben dyfodiad ein Harglwydd Iesu Grist i'r byd*, c.1832-42, published by John Jones, Llanrwst.

ment of harps. Unfortunately the gates of heaven bear a strong resemblance to the park gates of the local milord, constructed to keep the masses out, and they seem rather emphatically closed despite the general rejoicing. A less ambiguous triumphal image, probably inspired by Revelations, shows two angels with swords of flame protecting a sleeping child Jesus, about to be crowned, from a very unpleasant Devil who is vanquished below. John Jones used this block with several ballads.

James Cope's taste for surreal imagery found its most dramatic expression on the frontispiece to John Jones's *Hanes y Lleuad* (The Story of the Moon). In 1835 in the *New York Sun*, it was satirically suggested by R.A. Locke that the astronomer Sir John Herschell, working with a huge telescope in South Africa, had observed fantastic humanoid creatures with wings flying about on the surface of the moon. Not surprisingly, since it purported to come from such an eminent authority, the account caused a sensation and was regurgitated the world over in the popular press. This early piece of space fiction stimulated James Cope's imagination into producing what is certainly the most remarkable illustration of a Welsh-language text in the period.

A number of James Cope's pictures, including the *Adda ac Efa*, were copied by an unknown maker of woodblocks for the press of Isaac Thomas in Cardigan. They exemplify within Wales the process of transmission that carried a common iconography from one side of Europe to the other and to America. Yet the Cardigan prints have a highly distinctive naive style, both in the drawing of individual elements and in composition, which transforms the source material into original work. Isaac Thomas's output of large format ballad sheets was greater and more varied than that of John Jones. In addition to biblical subject matter, hymns and moralities, it also included murders and scandals, and depictions of state occasions. Isaac Thomas also produced more English-language and bilingual editions than John Jones, and presumably because of the press available to him, usually worked to a larger format.

Almost all of Isaac Thomas's woodcuts were done especially for him and are clearly by the same hand. That hand may have been his own, since the production of large ballad sheets seems to have stopped on his death in 1853, but could equally be the work of one of his printers or a carpenter. Their style suggests that they were not the work of a trained engraver working independently, and indeed no engraver was listed in the street directories for Cardigan for the period covered by the production of the prints.[8] Isaac Thomas kept files of his proofs and sometimes noted the

I GYMRY mwynion, de'wch heb ball,
Rho'wch eich clust fel dynion call;
Clywch riddfanau, oerion eiriau,
A gofidiau bachgen dall:
Darfu gweled goleu'r dydd,
Dirfawr ofnau arnaf sydd;
Gan fod t'lodi yn fy ngwasgu,
Pwy a wyr pa beth a fydd?

print runs, providing useful information about the scale of production. On 14 August 1840, for instance, Isaac Thomas printed 500 copies of a new ballad by Levi Gibbon of Monach, near Llanboidy, Carmarthenshire. The ballad itself is also precisely dated to January 24th and is unusually accompanied by a copyright warning. It complains of food shortages and high taxes. It was printed with three portraits, unrelated to the text and to a smaller format than usual, probably reflecting the limited resources available to the ballad singer who must have paid for its production. Levi Gibbon came to be known as Bachgen Dall Cwmfelin but had gone blind only shortly before this ballad was written:

All good WELSH people, gather round,
Listen now without a sound;
Hear my groaning, cold bemoaning,
In my blindness ever bound:
Not to see the light of day,
Hideous fears upon me prey;
Weighed down and poor, with heavy heart,
What will happen, who can say?

This original example is unusual since most of Isaac Thomas's ballads were fished from the large pool of material already published, and seem to have been the result of the printer's own entrepreneurship. Isaac

Hanes y Lleuad, by James Cope, c. 1836-42, published by John Jones, Llanrwst.

Myfyrdod ar y Bedd...,
published by Isaac
Thomas, Cardigan,
c.1835-53.

Thomas printed his copy of the central part of Cope's *Adda ac Efa* with Dafydd William's depressing *Colyn Angau*, for instance, and also used it to accompany *Myfyrdod ar y Cloc yn Taro*, with a cut of the return of the prodigal son. The grave is well represented in Isaac Thomas's productions. An anonymous *Myfyrdod ar y Bedd* is accompanied by a fine naive copy of a Catnach picture entitled *The Awful Death Bed of Caroline Johnstone*, an interesting transformation of a shocking individual story into a general warning to be prepared. The main image was accompanied by one of several smaller graveyard scenes owned by the printer.

Unlike John Jones, Isaac Thomas sometimes adopted the convention of creating funereal images by the setting of his texts. Both *Llef yr Amddifad...* (The Cry of the Destitute...) and the English-language equivalent, *Time & Eternity, and the Saints Sweet Home*, were preceded by texts printed in the shape of funerary urns expressing sentiments typified by Romans 14: "As by one man sin entered into the world, and death by sin; and so death passed upon all men, for that all have sinned." They are surmounted by graveyards. Both versions also include two statuesque ladies who appear in a wide variety of guises in Isaac Thomas's prints.

The popularity of this combination of dismal sentiments is difficult to understand, since the naive visual quality which now makes the prints so attractive is a retrospective perception and would certainly not have been a part of the motivation to buy the prints when they were new. Nevertheless, it is hard to believe that religious zeal was responsible for their popularity since such zeal might be expected to have been found in rather puritanical persons not inclined to the consumption of bowdlerised biblical texts. It may be—with such high rates of mortality (and especially child mortality)—that the purchase of prints of this kind became a part of mourning ritual. Towns in the period were subject to serious outbreaks of whooping cough and scarlet fever, and sometimes also cholera, as at Caernarfon in 1830 and again in 1848. The Welsh-language version of the print depicts both a mourning woman and a scene of reapers at work.

Some of Isaac Thomas's prints were made with children in mind, such as the hymn for the Sunday schools published with a cut of a mother and two small girls in a decorated border of foliage and flowers. The bold style of the Bible story prints will have appealed to the same audience, though probably not intended especially for them. Because Isaac Thomas was

Time & Eternity and the Saints' Sweet Home, published by Isaac Thomas, Cardigan, c.1835-53.

so dependent on outside sources both for his ballads and his pictures, the two seldom precisely matched on his publications, but with ingenuity he was able to make points coherently. He coupled *Daniel in the Lion's Den*, borrowed from Catnach, with R. Williams's *Myfyrdod ar Farwolaeth* and the fine *Goliath a Dafydd* with an anonymous ballad called *Tiriondeb Rhagluniaeth Duw* (The Tenderness of God's Providence). In this print, as in *Homeward bound for Canaan*, Isaac Thomas's style was at its most distinctive, with the large single images surrounded by massive borders of parallel lines and corner decorations. On *Homeward bound for Canaan* Isaac Thomas used a shipwreck, probably borrowed from a print depicting a particular incident, as an allegory. The ship has been allowed to founder despite the presence of the lighthouse. A more watchful ship passes by safely in the background:

Myfyrdod ar Farwolaeth...
published by Isaac
Thomas, Cardigan,
c. 1835-53.

We've join'd the Lord High Admiral's ship,
    His standard now is waving;
We'll range along across the deep;
    Sailors and Soldiers saving.
      Canaan! great Canaan!
    Starboard for the land of Canaan;
    "Keep a good look out there—fore and aft;"
    Will you hail for the land of Canaan!

Only in one surviving example does the Cardigan engraver seem to have ventured on an original composition for a particular text—the parable of the rich glutton and Lazarus the beggar. The story, from Luke 16, is quoted in full under the picture, followed by Dafydd William's ballad which recounts the same story but much embroidered with familiar and realistic detail, in the manner of a sermon. The engraver followed the same principle, transferring the image from a middle eastern, biblical context, to Cardiganshire in the 1840s. The self-satisfied but doomed gentleman emerges from his respectable villa and passes by Lazarus without a glance. His stone and slate-roofed residence, typical of the area, looks modest enough in retrospect, but in comparison to the single story thatched hovels of most of the rural population, would have seemed distinctly posh at the time:

    The King of fear came to him,
        To knock upon his gate;
    His heart it shook in terror,
        As he announced his fate;
    In vain his endless wailing,
        The pain tore at his skin,
    His rank and wealth were useless,
        Reduced to nought, for sin.

    Behind him, now, his parlour,
        His palace, oh so grand,
    His treasured hours forgotten,
        Torn from his empty hand;
    Cold worms now eat his body,
        His soul for ever sent,
    Below to fire and brimstone,
        The hapless way he went.

In hell he woke the next day,
    Though much against his will,
In fright, surprise and terror,
    He waits there, silent, still:
Eternal flames bind round him,
    His feet in chains of steel,
No one can hear his moaning,
    His miserable appeal.

Goliath a Dafydd,
published by Isaac
Thomas, Cardigan,
c. 1835-53.

And when he looked above him,
　　From th'hideous lake of fate,
He saw the beggar standing,
　　Who once stood at his gate,
With golden harp, in glory,
　　Before the gleaming throne,
In shining robes of triumph,
　　A golden crown, his own.

The theme of heaven and hell as the world-turned-upside-down was a favourite of those writing for the moral instruction of the populace. The promise of eternal damnation for the abuse of good fortune in the earthly life seems to have been considered by most eighteenth and nineteenth-century priests and ministers sufficient sustenance for the downtrodden.

Isaac Thomas issued accounts of murders with illustrations in large format. Most had a Welsh connection, if sometimes tenuous, such as the murder of Jane Jones in Putney in 1842. He used a combination of borrowed images to relate the story, cartoon strip fashion, including a keyed block of the stable where the event took place. The unfortunate lady had been disembowelled, and had her legs, arms and head cut off. The events were described in detail in prose, followed by an anonymous ballad. John Jones, on the other hand, issued only a very few murders in large format. This may be because James Cope was disinclined to illustrate them and his stock of second-hand blocks were mostly too small to look effective. Only one example, possibly by Cope, is known, and it would not be difficult to account for this exception since the murder involved supernatural forces which would have appealed to Cope's gothic imagination. Having left a pub late one dark night in November 1837, a farmer was found dead the next morning at the foot of a ravine on the road between Maentwrog and Llandecwyn. The farmer's body was mangled and mutilated, but there was still money in his pocket, leading the coroner's inquest to conclude, with a rather limited view of human motivation, that he had not died by human hand. The engraver's speculation was that a huge devilish animal, part dog, part hare and with cloven hoofs, had been responsible:

Daeth Brenin dychryniadau,
I guro wrth gaerau'r gwr,
Fe wnaeth i'w galon grynu,
A thoddi fel y dw'r;
Gwaith ofer oedd och'neidio,
Ac angau'n rhwygo'i gnawd
Heb brisio'i waed na'i uchder,
Dim mwy na'r begger tlawd.

Fe orfu gado'i barlwr,
A'i swccwr gwych a'i blâs,
Heb gofio'i werthfawr oriau,
Nes treulio rhai'n i ma's;
Ei gorph yn fwyd i'r pryfed,
A'i enaid hirfod maith,
I lawr i'r tân trag'wyddol,
Annedwydd oedd ei daith.

Yn uffern fe ddihunodd,
O'i anfodd, nid o'i fodd,
Mewn dychryn mawr a syndod,
Cyn 'nabod dim b'le'r o'dd:
Mae dan drag'wyddol gwlwm,
Mewn cadwyn dan y clo,
'Does neb a'i clyw yn griddfan,
Y truan, trwm ei dro.

Pan cododd ei olygon,
Yn yr echryslon lyn,
Fe welodd y Cardottyn,
Fu wrth ei borth cyn hyn,
Yn canu a'i delyn auraidd,
O flaen yr orsedd wen,
Mewn disclaer wisgoedd gwynion,
A'i goron ar ei ben.

GALARNAD

Er cof am Amaethwr parchus oedd yn byw yn Ngogleddbarth Sir Feirionydd,
yr hwn a gafwyd wedi marw rhwng Maentwrog a Llandecwyn Tach. 25, 1837.

1
Gwrandewch yn syn ar hyn o hanes,
Mae genyf gyffes drist i'w chael,
Mae wedi bod yn nôd anedwydd,
Yn Sir Feirionydd hylwydd hael;
O bob hanesion trymion welais
Neu a glywais a'm dwy glust
Dyma'r ddamwain fwyaf chwerw,
Mi ddwcda'n groesaw Duw sy'n dyst,

2
Mae einoes dyn mor ansertenol,
Fel nas gwyr neb o ddynol ryw,
Pa awr pa funud y terfyna,
Pa beth a'i bwria o dir y byw;
Ein dyledswydd yw gweddio
Ar Dduw tra byddom yn y byd,
Am iddo gadw meibion dynion,
Rhag peryglon ar bob pryd

3
Yr oedd yn byw gerllaw Maentwrog
Wr cyfoethog enwog iawn,
A chanddo dai ac aur ac arian,
A meddinnau llydain llawn,
A'i berth'nasau yn gysurus,
Yn bobl barchus yn y byd,
Roedd ganddo ddigon ar ei gyfer
Heb ofni prinder ar bob pryd.

4
Y pedwerydd dydd ar hugain
O Dachwedd ydoedd yn ddi os,
O dy Tafarn y cychwynodd
Adre' am un ar ddeg o'r nos
Prun bynag oedd ai meddw ai sobor
Fe ga'dd ei wobr am ei waith,
Daeth cennad angau yn ddychrynllyd
I'w yru i dragwyddolfyd maith.

5
'Roedd ei ffordd i fyned adre'
Trwy goed a chregiau siwrnau syn,
A cholli'r llwybr ddarfu a moedro,
Mae'n hawdd i ni ddarlunio hyn,
Rhwng Maentwrog a Llandecwyn
Mae lleoedd gerwin bron i gyd,
Trwy ryw foddion anarferol
Ca'dd fyned i'r anfarwol fyd.

6
O herwydd na chyrhaeddodd adre,
Ei nith y borau'n ddiau ddaeth
I'r Ty Tafarn lle cychwynodd,
Am ei Hewythr holi a wnaeth;
Ni wydda'i rhai'ny ddim o'i hanes
Nad oedd ef gartref, dyma'r gwir,
Wrth chwilio am dano ei gorff a gaf.
Er braw a syndod i bob Sir.   (wyd,

7
Ei gorff a'i ddillad ydoedd yno
Wedi eu dryllio yn arw eu trefn,
Yn ochr ceunant 'roedd yn waeledd
Fel yn gorwedd ar ei gefn,
A'i bocedau ddarfynt chwilio,
A chaed ei ariau ganddo i gyd,
A ffaelodd cwest y Coroner farnu
I ddynion ei ddibenu o'r byd.

8
Yr oedd hi'n galed yn ddi gelu
Ar bawb ga'dd brofi'r cuini caeth,
Fu yn y golwg gyda'r gelain
Wrth feddwl am y ddamwain ddaeth,
Wrth iddynt gario'i gorff i'r gweryd
O ! mor drymllyd oedd y tro. (dychryn
Roedd yno bawb mewn braw a
Wrth gofio hyn mewn bryn a bro,

9
Yn awr mae pawb a'i reswm ganddo
A mawr y swn am dano sy,
A phawb yn siarad 'nol ei anian
Am yr erchyll ddamwain ddu,
Pa fodd y trengodd pwy all dystio,
Pa beth fu'n darnio corph y dyn,
A pha hyd ybu yn poeni
'Does neb wyr hyny ond Duw ei hun.

10
Nid wyf fi am arfer cabledd,
Na chodi'r un ddi sylwedd sen,
Ond wrth ei ffrwythau medd'r Ysrythur
Felly profir beth yw'r pren;
O herwydd hyn o hanes hynod
Mawr yw'r braw a'r syndod sydd ;
Mae ei geraint a'i berth'nasau
Yn wylo dagrau a'u bronau'n brudd.

11
Megys tarth neu wlith y borau
Ydyw dyddiau einioes dyn,
Pa awr pa funud gwna derfynu,
'Does neb wyr hyny ond Duw ei hun,
Boed i ni geisio gras yn groeso
Trwy weddio ar Dduw yn ddwys
Am i'n eueidiau gael trugaredd
Cyn rhoddi'n cyrff i'r geufedd gwys.

12
Mae'n bryd is wybren ini sobri,
A throi o ddifri i grefu ar Grist,
Am ein puro a'n gwneud yn barod,
Cyn marwol ddyrnod trallod trist,
Yr Arglwydd nefol a'n cymhwyso,
Fel y byddo ei waith yn ben
I fyn'd i ganu i wlad gogoniant
Yn y mwyniant byth AMEN.

YWAIN MEIRION-

LLANRWST, ARGRAFFWYD GAN J. JONES.

Now each one has his explanation
And all the tongues to talk are freed,
Each one can speak his mind or fancy
About the fearsome, dreadful deed.
The cause of death there's none can witness
Nor say what thing has split his bones
How long his dreadful agony
Just God alone in Heaven knows.

The attribution of this woodcut to Cope is complicated by the appearance two years earlier, in 1835, of the earliest illustrations by Ellis Owen Ellis on a publication by John Jones. When he cut the blocks for *Bywyd Turpin Leidr,* a translation by John Evans (known as I.D. Ffraid) of the story of Dick Turpin, Ellis had been only 22 and still studying art. There were six illustrations, of which four were certainly by Ellis. Closely similar to them are blocks on four murder ballads of about the same period, the earliest probably issued in 1833. Richard Williams, Dic Dywyll, wrote the history of the murder of Mary Pemberton by Samuel Thorley. Ellis also produced a set of blocks to illustrate *Hanes Dic Siôn Dafydd* by Jac Glanygors, one of the most popular ballads of the period, first published in 1811.

Ellis Owen Ellis was a radical with an enthusiasm for the popular press, but apart from his woodcut illustration to *Hyfforddwr y Ffermwr* (The Farmer's Instructor), published by John Jones about 1850, and his late political cartoons for *Y Punch Cymraeg* (The Welsh Punch), few of his woodcuts and wood engravings have, as yet, been identified. This may be because he worked mostly in Liverpool for the English-language press. A number of abortive projects have survived as drawings that were never translated into prints. The most celebrated of these, *Oriel y Beirdd* (The Gallery of Bards), is known only from a photograph. The inspiration

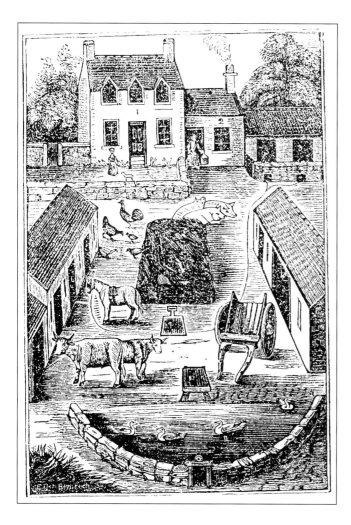

Os morwyn oedd hi'n myned yno,
Rhaid i ni gael gwyro at y gwir,
Hi gollodd, mae'n resyn dal sylw,
Yr enw cyn pen hir;
Dechreuodd wisgo sidanau,
Perwigau o bob lliwiau i'w gwellhau,
Pe gwelsech chwi'r aur wrth ei chopa,
Yn chwipio mewn cadair a dau...

was clearly the kind of public art for national buildings brought to public attention in the period by the reconstruction of the Houses of Parliament in London. In the absence of an appropriate Welsh building, Ellis Owen Ellis intended to issue his gallery of the "literary celebrities of the Principality" as a print. The cartoon was exhibited at the London Eisteddfod of 1855 and set off a parochial argument which rumbled on until the artist's death in 1861, the print still unissued. Some southerners took offence at the omission of poets such as Islwyn and Gwilym Tawe from the ranks of the great and the good. Clearly Gwilym Tawe himself was not offended, since, according to tradition, he bought the cartoon for a hundred guineas.[9]

Two other of Ellis's abortive projects provide a rare opportunity to study the preparatory work of a popular engraver. Like *Dic Siôn Dafydd*, the ballad *Betti o Lansanffraid* was written by Jac Glanygors, and with a similar message. Dic Siôn Dafydd became the archetype of those Welsh people who denied their national origins in order to gain social advancement in England, or within Wales, who aped the social affectations of the English for the same reason. Betti became upwardly mobile by using her good looks and also suffered a fall. *The Book of Welsh Ballads, illustrated in outline* was probably drawn by Ellis Owen Ellis in the mid-1840s and consists of seven illustrations of Betti's rise from feeding the pigs to being courted in London, followed by her chastened, but not chaste, return home:

> A virgin she was when she went there,
>   But we must, I fear, hold to the truth,
> It's sad that I now have to tell you,
>   She lost that name, still in her youth;
> Bright silks to improve her appearance,
>   And wigs of such fine coloured hair,

Frontispiece to *Hyfforddwr y Ffermwr*, by Ellis Owen Ellis, published by John Jones, Llanrwst, c.1850.

Drawings for *Betti o Lansanffraid*, by Ellis Owen Ellis, c.1845.

113

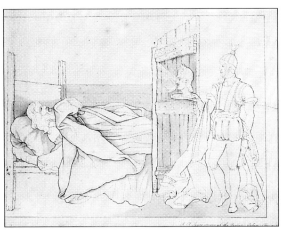

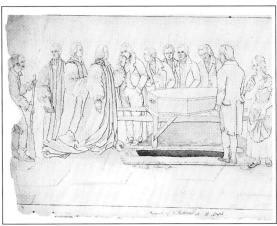

If you saw the gold on her forehead,
Fly past in her carriage and pair...

There is no evidence to suggest why Ellis failed to engrave the pictures and have them published, along with the very similar *Illustrated Life of Richard Robert Jones, Aberdaron*, done in 1844. Dic Aberdaron, who had died the year before, already had by far the largest popular iconography of any Welsh person of the first half of the nineteenth century, and would have been a very popular subject.

The essence of the public fascination with Dic Aberdaron was the contrast between his exceptional mental abilities and his filthy appearance. He was believed to be able to read more than a dozen languages, but was known to the genteel ladies of Liverpool, before whom he was exhibited by his patron William Roscoe, as "the learned pig".[10] The contrast was heightened by the visual metaphor of a handsome head poking out from layers of rotting and dishevelled clothes. Not surprisingly, nearly all the texts about Dic Aberdaron were accompanied by pictures. Intellectual interest revolved around the contrast between his facility in the translation of languages and his inability to grasp the meaning of what he had translated. The fascination was deepened by his visionary dreams of such subjects as the head of Herod and the harp of David.

William Roscoe attempted a scholarly analysis of this contradictory phenomenon, published in 1822[11] and prefaced with a Byronic portrait by William Clements, suggesting the innate genius that the author sensed burning deep within. Clements's second portrait was a wood engraving, less romantic but still emphasising the heroic head. However, as early as 1823, Dic Aberdaron had also been presented to the public in his low-brow popular character. The miniature painter Burt, in addition to a lost

Richard Robert Jones *the wonderful Linguist.*
born at Aberdaron, Caernarvonshire now living in Liverpool
Drawn Engraved & published by A.R.Burt. Miniature painter Chester. May 30. 1823.

Richard Robert Jones — of Aberdaron, in Caernarvonshire — as he appeared at Beaumaris Eisteddfod.

Richard Robert Jones, the wonderful Linguist..., by A.R. Burt, 1823.

Richard Robert Jones, Dic Aberdaron, at the Beaumaris Eisteddfod of 1832, by John Orlando Parry.

portrait, produced a full length of Dic as seen on the streets of Liverpool which was etched and sold at 1s plain and 1/6d coloured. It was accompanied by a short biography entitled "Craniology", in deference to the scientific interest of the phenomenon. It was in this character that Dic became a legend. He was sought out by artists. William Roos's portrait of him is among his finest works and one which he copied several times. An otherwise unknown painter called Richard Williams made two portraits, and John Orlando Parry came from London to draw him. A portrait bust was set up in the Liverpool Mechanics' Institute.

William Clements produced his third image of Dic Aberdaron in 1837, a full length including the books, French horn and tall hat for which he was best known. It was this portrait that was most widely distributed and which formed the basis of most of the cheap prints produced after Dic's death in 1843. Hugh Humphreys, the Caernarfon publisher, was quick to respond to the sad event with *Hanes Bywyd Dic Aberdaron* (The Story of the Life of Dic Aberdaron) the following year, subsequently reprinted several times and translated into English with Clements' engraving as a frontispiece. In these later versions, Dic is proficient in 35 languages. The block was borrowed by Humphreys from its owner, Joseph Mayer of Liverpool, in 1848.[12] However, the paper cover of the first edition had carried a woodcut which although similar to Clements' also included Dic's cat and a harp. On grounds of style it seems likely to be the work of Ellis Owen Ellis, though whether it was Hugh Humphreys whom Ellis intended to publish his *Illustrated Life...* that same year is not clear. There are twelve drawings, beginning with the funeral and including the visionary dreams. The details of the iconography suggest that Ellis Owen Ellis may have had access to Dic's own hand-written accounts, rather than the published versions. As we have seen, Ellis spent much of his working life in Liverpool where he would have had every chance to get to know his subject personally.

A WELSH CORPORATION MEETING

The Corporation of Swansea met at their Guildhall Nov 21st 1767 when Gabriel Powell Recorder, Steward to the Duke of Beaufort, brought up an Act by Authority snatched out of the Hands of Mr Padley a Paper...

The STEWARD

Swansea is a poor Town mostly inhabited by Copper men and Colliers, but as well paved as most Country Towns are I know of no Theatre there, I may have heard of one, I never was at it. G.P. Horse Comm Apr 19 1767

Gabriel Powell.

116

VI A view from the inside—
Welsh political comment

The absence of a national politics, and even of substantial urban centres in which the machinations of local power might give rise to both subject matter and a home audience for popular satirical prints, prevented their development in Wales until the 1780s.

Thomas Pennant did not need to sell his prints but the proximity of his home in Flintshire to the urban centres of Chester and Shrewsbury provided a show-place for them among a population well acquainted with the characters depicted, since the debate was aired in the local press. Urban centres of this sort, with a substantial English-speaking population and a local press to feed it, were then only beginning to develop in Wales itself. The first weekly newspaper, *The Cambrian*, appeared in 1806 in Swansea. It is, therefore, not surprising that the earliest cartoons to deal with exclusively local political issues in Wales came out of the growing pains of that same town. In 1787, moves were afoot to improve both the harbour and the paving and lighting of Swansea. For reasons of self-interest, elements on the corporation not only opposed the developments but authorised the expenditure of £500 of corporation money to finance their opposition to the requisite Act of Parliament. However, the resolution to grant the money was passed only after a heated debate culminating in a most undignified scuffle. Gabriel Powell, the Recorder (who was 81 years old at the time), had snatched a paper from the hands of another member, and "his son, Thomas Powell a Clargyman and Alderman afterwards knocked down Mr. Chas. Collins an Emminent Surgeon... and while on the ground most malignently and cowerdly kicked him in ye Breast, The father seased Mr. Collins wig...", according to the caption of the cartoon of the event drawn by Moses Harris.

Gabriel Powell subsequently gave evidence before the parliamentary committee dealing with the bill. His vain attempts to resist change were satirized in a second cartoon by Moses Harris, entitled *The Steward*. Standing in a conspicuously unpaved and befouled street, he testified that "Swansea is a poor town mostly inhabited by Copper men and Colliers; but as well paved as most Country Towns are." On the other side of the street stands the recently established Swansea Theatre, a supplementary dig at the reactionary and puritanical Recorder. "I know no theatre there," he says, "I may have heard of one: never was at it."

There is no other record of the cartoonist.[1] Nevertheless, there may have been other Swansea satires at an early date, since—contrary to Powell's evidence to Parliament—the town was neither poor nor exclusively occupied by copper men and colliers. There was, in fact, a substantial fashionable community there, especially during the summer months. A far larger number of artists and art teachers have been recorded visiting Swansea than any other town in Wales in the period,[2] to take advantage of this market. Among them for a few years around 1770 was Giuseppi Marchi, friend of Thomas Jones, Pencerrig, William Parry, and no doubt others of the Welsh circle in London. It was Marchi who engraved Berridge's portrait of Evan Lloyd, surely not a coincidental choice. In 1809, a cartoon was published in London concerning one of the Swansea socialites. *Venus a la Coquelle; or the Swan-sea Venus* has been variously interpreted but seems to represent Ann Hatton, known as "Ann of Swansea".[3] Ann was the sister of the actress Sarah Siddons, and came to Swansea to live about 1799, where she and her husband kept the bathing house until 1806 when she moved to Cydweli. The cartoon probably celebrates her return to Swansea in 1809, paid by her family on condition she kept 150 miles from London, as a result of the rather scandalous reputation she had acquired there. In Swansea she wrote her many substantial novels. The caricature has the spoof signature "Shon ap Shones" in the tradition of the seventeenth-century woodcuts.

As we have seen, radical political tracts emanating from Wales or written specifically for Welsh people, were extremely rare in the eighteenth century. The interlude *Barn ar egwyddorion llywodraeth*, built around William Jones's *Principles of Government*, seems to be the earliest example, followed soon after by *Seren Tan Gwmmwl* (A Star under a Cloud), 1795 and *Toriad y Dydd* (The Break of Day), 1797, by John Jones, Jac Glanygors, and based on the ideas of Tom Paine. Jac Glanygors was a founder member of the Cymreigyddion Society, established in 1795, the only one of the Welsh

A Welsh Corporation Meeting, by Moses Harris, 1787.

The Steward, by Moses Harris, 1787.

117

Venus a la Coquelle; _ or _ the Swansea Venus,

Venus a la Coquelle, or the
Swansea Venus, by Shon
ap Shones, published by
Hannah Humphrey,
London, 1809.

societies set up as a political club. His revolutionary instincts and the fact that the Cymreigyddion operated (unlike the other societies) through the medium of the Welsh language, brought it under suspicion. Jac had to flee London and hide in Wales for some time. His revolutionary fervour went much further than that of most of his colleagues, but Thomas Roberts, Llwyn'rhudol, also participated in the pamphleteering of the period, publishing his *Cwyn yn erbyn Gorthrymder* (A Complaint against Oppression) in 1798. The pamphlet was an attack on the established church and especially on its maintenance by tithes, but in that unstable period any attack on one of the pillars of the state seemed seditious to conservatives, which is why Llwyn'rhudol felt obliged to protest his loyalty in the text. *Cwyn yn erbyn Gorthrymder* was remarkable for including the first political cartoon with a caption in the Welsh language. An obese and aggressive priest is on tour, extracting tithes in the form of pigs, geese and chickens, from his hard-working parishioners. Two of them bend their knees before him while an inscription on a milestone reminds us of the 10th commandment: Thou shalt not covet... anything that is thy neighbour's. Above and below the cartoon two couplets by Jac Glanygors are quoted:

Priest.   No place in heaven for the poor
                  Unless they pay their tithes!

Old woman.   The good life is, I suppose,
                   The burden of the priest.

The iconography of this scene is not peculiarly Welsh. The English series "Bowles and Carver's Caricatures", for instance, published in the 1760s, included a farmyard scene with a parson claiming his tithe under the title *A Satire on the Clergy*. Nevertheless, the question as to why the people should maintain a church to which they had no allegiance was coming to have national associations in Wales. The success of the Nonconformist denominations preaching in the Welsh language (brought into sharp focus by the secession of the Methodists in 1811), encouraged the perception of the Church of England as a foreign church, indifferent to the needs of Welsh people nominally in its care.

Offeiriad. Nid Ne, ydyw lle, dyn llwm,
Oni ddaw i ni, ddegwm'.

Yr Henwraig. Eich bygad yw, delygwn,
Byd da, yn y bywyd hwn. Glanygors.

Cwyn yn erbyn
Gorthrymder, by an
unknown engraver, 1798.

Neither the designer nor the engraver of Llwyn'rhudol's print are known, and it does not seem to have been issued separately from the pamphlet. It is also an isolated Welsh-language example—no other satires in the Welsh language would appear until well after the end of the French wars. The radical enthusiasm of the Cymreigyddion was soon curtailed by the turn of events in France, which brought Napoleon rather than Liberty to the fore, and its energy continued to decline after the war until the late 1820s. However, in 1828, Hugh Hughes joined the society, at a time when freedom—though not revolution—was again the cry. Jac Glanygors was dead, but Llwyn'rhudol was still an active member. Under his influence, and mindful of the society's tradition, Hughes and his radical colleagues, especially Thomas Edwards, Caerfallwch, and Griffith Davies, revitalised the Cymreigyddion, in the belief that education and the parliamentary system could together deliver change both in Britain as a whole and in matters of particular concern to Wales. The period of Hughes's activity in the Cymreigyddion, from 1828 to 1832, saw the emancipation of Catholics and the passing of the Great Reform Bill. Looking to the continent, radicals were excited by the freedom movement in Greece and the 1830 revolution in Paris. They had high expectations and were mindful, as ever, of the mythology that linked them in particular, as Welsh people, to the idea of British freedom. They admired the English popular press and sought to imitate it in the Welsh language, setting up the radical monthly Y Cymro, described as "that revolutionary periodical", by an indignant clergyman in Bala.

Y Cymro was edited by a group of Cymreigyddion, including Hugh Hughes, but the most obvious contribution of the engraver was the allegorical image of the new nation printed on the first page of the first number in January, 1830. Subsequently it was printed on the paper covers of each issue. This wood engraving was the most ambitious of Hughes's many images of the word as the medium of personal and national progress. The new Welshman sits, not reading but writing—that is to say, actively participating in the democratic spirit of the age, in improving the human condition. Behind him are symbols of national identity and progress. The image was interpreted in detail in the accompanying text: "Our readers see a plain Welshman composing an issue of Y CYMRO...." Cultural origins are represented by the Eisteddfod chair in which he sits and by a cromlech. The new Wales emerges in harmony with the old—as a single landscape—represented by a steamship and factories. This is the only specific image of industry in any of Hughes's surviving works. A less well chosen symbol of the future, perhaps, was the hot air balloon. This image of a Welsh renaissance represented a radical though not party-political agenda. In the pages of Y Cymro and by petitioning parliament, the Cymreigyddion and their supporters in Wales itself campaigned for the immediate appointment of

Y Cymro.

Rhif. 1.]   IONAWR, 1830.   [Cyf. I.

EGLURHAD O'R CERFIAD.

Ein darllenyddion a welant Gymro gwladaidd (plaïn) yn cyfansoddi Rhifyn o'r Cymro. Gwelir yn y pellder Gwch Angerdd, (steam vessel,) yn nghyd a llongau ereill; ac hefyd gweithfa fasnachol (factory,) a mwyndai tawdd, i'r dyben o arddangos y bydd i'r Cyhoeddiad roddi dealldwriaeth hysbysol ar faterion masnachol, diwydrwydd, a chynnyrch y wlad. Yr awyr-ged, (air balloon,) a ddengys y bwriedir difyru yn gystal a dysgu yr anghyfarwydd. Y Castell a hysbysa y darllenydd, y geill ddysgwyl yn y gwaith hwn erthyglau ar yr ymdrechiadau gorchestol a wnaed gan ein Henafiaid i gadw meddiant -o, ac amddiffyn " Gwyllt Walia." Tra yr adgoffa y Gromlech iddo y caiff ei dueddgarwch henafiaethol ei boddâu. Yr Arddwr yn aredig, yn nghyd a'r gwartheg corniog, a addawant na chaiff hwsmonaeth ac amaethyddiaeth eu hebargofi. Y Belen

Y Cymro Newydd, by Hugh Hughes, 1830.

Welsh bishops and for the eventual disestablishment of the Church of England, for Welsh-speaking judges in the courts, for a Welsh university and the righting of numerous social wrongs.

Through Hugh Hughes, the radical tradition of this small group of London Welsh people was linked to developments in Wales itself. For the second time, Hughes's presence in Wales would coincide with an outburst of activity in the popular press. In 1832 he left London and by 1834 was established in Caernarfon. Between that year and 1843 came political cartoons by James Cope, the first Welsh-language weekly newspaper, and the first Welsh satirical periodical, all emanating from the north-west of the country. In addition to Hughes and Cope, a number of other radical and Nonconformist intellectuals moved to Caernarfon. William Williams, Caledfryn, became minister of Pendre Independent chapel, his career and that of Hughes having in common the distinction of a dispute with John Elias which resulted in their parting company with the Methodists. They had probably known each other at least as early as 1820. In 1835, they established together a fortnightly radical newspaper, stimulated by what they regarded as the subversion of *Seren Gomer* by a new conservative

120

William Williams, Caledfryn, by John Thomas, c.1860-7.

editor. *Y Seren Ogleddol* (The Northern Star) was printed by Josiah Thomas Jones, Caledfryn's predecessor at Pendre. The political activism of Caledfryn and J.T. Jones did not make for a quiet life in the chapel, and indeed culminated in a schism. Josiah Thomas Jones was eventually forced to leave Caernarfon when a paternity suit, cooked up between conservative enemies of the printer and a prostitute, caused a great scandal. Jones was publicly supported by Hugh Hughes, Caledfryn, Christmas Evans and others, and the suit was dismissed in court.[4] Nevertheless, Jones departed for the industrial south under a cloud, where, in Merthyr and Aberdare he found a more amenable environment for his views. He established his own newspaper, *Y Gwron,* and continued to print ballads, illustrating them for many years with some of Hugh Hughes's stock of wood blocks which he seems to have acquired in the early 1830s.

In 1836, *Y Seren Ogleddol* evolved into *Y Papyr Newydd Cymraeg,* edited and published by Hugh Hughes alone, largely written by him, and since he and Caledfryn owed J.T. Jones money, also printed by him on a new press at his home in Church Street. The first Welsh-language weekly newspaper lasted 18 months before Hughes retired from the fray, exhausted, having failed to secure a sufficient readership.

It seems impossible that Hughes and Caledfryn did not know James Cope, though, strangely, no references to him in their correspondence have come to light. About 1834, Cope designed two anti-Tory cartoons, *Blwyddyn Newydd Dda i John Bull* (A Happy New Year to John Bull), and *Y Tories yn cael eu cymeryd adref at eu teulu* (The Tories taken home to their family). Cope's John Bull did not symbolise the jingoistic Englishman but rather a disappointed middle class, who were not seeing the change in their circumstances that the more optimistic among them had hoped would rapidly follow parliamentary reform. The Devil, the guardian of the establishment, has set his children—the monarchy, the church, the army and a host of place-men, unmoved by the widening of the franchise—on John Bull's back, causing an intolerable strain.[5] The Welsh-speaking John Bull draws the weight of Tory oppression and the church tithes which increasingly symbolised it, along by the ankles. The figures on his back were keyed to a text printed above. The same image later appeared on another print, without the Devil but still in the company of his portly companion, who refers to the New Poor Law, dating the cartoons to between 1834 and 1836 when tithes were commuted. In place of the prose captions of the earlier version, John Jones printed an unusual ballad

Lluniedydd dillyn ydyw,
Carwn ei waith, cywrain yw.
Gan Ellis ni gawn eilun,
O un llaw ni chawn well llun.
Pwy fydd hwyr i arwyrain,
Ei luniau gwych ar lèn gain?

Blwyddyn newydd dda i John Bull, by James Cope, c. 1834-6.

by Ywain Meirion which runs against the generally cautious and conservative tone of his work. As we have seen, in 1839 the poet would criticise the mischievous Chartists of Llanidloes, Merthyr and Newport, but in *Cwynfan John Bull* (John Bull's Lament) he bemoaned the lot of the downtrodden people:

> My condition gets sadder, I barely can suffer
> The burden put on me—my pocket is empty,
> Though I work long and lonely in terrible weather;
> Deceit and oppression bear down on the nation,
> It gets worse by the day for the farmers who pay.
> For every new law, unhappy our cry...

It seems certain that Ywain Meirion wrote his ballad after seeing *Blwyddyn Newydd Dda i John Bull,* either inspired by it or paid by John Jones or James Cope to write, which would explain the radical tone. The internal evidence of the ballad is conclusive about this order of events since it describes the cartoon in every detail:

> It's I who am slaving and working with bare hands,
> While others grow fatter, in sadness I stand;
> In dark and foul weather 'gainst the world I must fight,
> The idle to keep in their parlours so bright;
> This numberless pack, they bear down on my back
> A disorderly rabble, they babble and clack,
> The great round mill-stone wears me down to the bone,
> And the weights on my boots drag me back like black roots,
> Each hour after hour, the burden increases
> Reform we demanded—a Bill they conceded;
> What good did it do but my chains to renew?
> They burden the people, they are all robbing you.

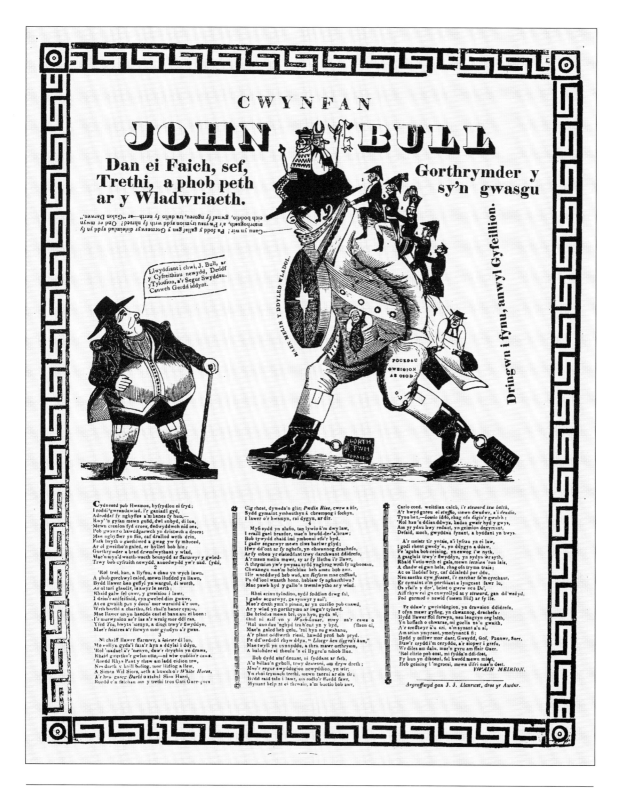

We have noted the close relationship between visual artists and poets in highbrow intellectual circles in eighteenth-century London, and later, in Wales itself, between artisan painters and the *beirdd gwlad*. Ywain Meirion's ballad on the theme of James Cope's *Cwynfan John Bull* was by no means a unique example of a poet responding to visual imagery. In 1855, Siôn Wyn o Eifion would write a eulogy to Ellis Owen Ellis's cartoon *Oriel y Beirdd*, casting a puritanical eye over one shoulder:

A limner, accomplished,
Refined, his work revered,
No idol from Ellis' hand
No better from an artist, grand.
To praise, what poet would shirk,
In fair words his fine work?

Cwynfan John Bull by James Cope, c. 1834-6.

123

Ellis produced the celebrated portrait of Siôn Wyn, *Y Bardd yn ei Wely* (The Bard in his Bed), for the frontispiece to his collected works. The tradition was carried into the twentieth century in a variety of poetic responses to Curnow Vosper's *Salem*.[6]

James Cope's political cartoons were printed by John Jones at Llanrwst rather than in Caernarfon by Josiah Thomas Jones, but since Cope paid for the earlier two himself—in the manner of the ballad singers—this may reflect no more than technical or perhaps financial considerations.

Y Tories yn cael eu cymeryd adref at eu teulu is undoubtedly James Cope's masterpiece, combining the gothic vigour of the woodcut tradition with the sophistication of the English intaglio cartoons. The Devilish imagery was ancient, carried into Welsh-language material in the mid-eighteenth century on ballad sheets such as *Gwrthwynebwch Ddiawl...* (Resist the Devil...), printed by Elizabeth Adams at Chester. Cope's reworking of it was elegant in design, and clear and sharp in technique. The Devil's servant Belphegor carries fifteen assorted Tory priests, placemen and politicians home to his master. Lucifer is less than satisfied, given the numbers at large:

> Hey ho, What have we here? says Lucifer;
> Fifteen TORIES, says Belphegor.
> How so? says the King, only fifteen, when they used to come in by the hundred.
> Have you not been out three days, Sir, and yet brought me only fifteen more?

The precise occasion for the publication of this print remains obscure, but it seems to be associated with British rather than Welsh politics, since the Duke of Wellington, with a gibbet on his hat, is clearly identifiable hanging on to Belphegor's tail. Hugh Hughes and Caledfryn must surely have been delighted. Nevertheless, the years after 1834 may have seen a difference of opinion between them, if the evidence of Cope's next cartoons can be taken as reflecting his own opinions rather than those of a patron.

In the mid-1830s the temperance movement rapidly gained strength in Wales, dividing communities into supporters of moderate drinking or teetotallers. Hughes and Caledfryn were moderates, and by 1836, Caledfryn was expressing the view that the teetotallers were manifesting such an excess of zeal that their anti-alcohol sentiments were supplanting Christianity as a religion. He attacked the zealots in a pamphlet, *Cymedroldeb a Llwyrymataliad; Sylwadau ar y Ddwy Egwyddor* (Moderation

CAN DDIRWESTOL,

SEF

YMFFROST

SYR JOHN HEIDDEN.

Cenir ar "Poor Jack."

Gwrandewch, y Cymry Bon,
Mi draethaf rai o'm campau,
Fy enw yw Syr John,
Gwr llawn wyf o bob castiau ;
Gan bawb mewn gwlad a thref,
Yr ydwyf yn dderbyniol :
Nid oes o dan y nef
Bendefig mor urddasol.

Mae genyf ddeiliaid fyrdd
Ym mhob rhyw le o tanaf ;
Ac ymddwyn ym mhob ffyrdd
At y rhai hyn y byddaf ;
Bywoliaeth fras bob awr
Sydd genyf i'r goreuon,
Hyd nes, wrth rodio' r llawr,
Y siglant megys Eglon.

Mi wisgais deulu rhai
Mewn porphor a sidanau,
Am roddi lle'n eu tai,
I'm baros hwyr a boreu :
A chodais ar ei farch,
Do, lawer un o'r domen—
Am hyn 'rwyt yn cael parch,
A'm galw'n Syr John Heidden

Mi fedraf fyw' yn llys
A byw'n y bwthyn gwaelaf—
Rhoes llawer un ei grys
Oddi am ei gefn am danaf —
Gwnaeth llawer gwr ei wraig
Er mwyn fy nhgael i'w feddiant,
Mor lom ac ydyw'r graig
Sy'n ymyl blaen y Pennant.

Mae gan fy neiliaid blant
Cyffelyb i fwganod,
O herwydd bod eu chwant
Tu ag ataf fi yn ormod;
Ni chlywir neb o'r rhain
O herwydd hyn yn cwyno,
Ac nid yw byw yn fain
Un amser yn eu blino.

Bydd pob oferddyn ffol,
A llawer budrog anllad,
Yn dyfod ar fy ol
Yn glym eu cerddediad;
A lladron penau ffyrdd
Yn wastad fydd i'm dilyn ;
O'r rhai'n anfonais fyrdd
I feirw yn y tenyu.

Mae rhai yn dweyd fy mod
Yn un or lladron penaf
Fy hun o dan y rhod ,
Er maint o serch sydd ataf;
Ac hefyd y mae cwyn
Fy mod yn llofrudd gerwin ;
Ond lladd yn ddigon mwyn
Y byddaf yn gyffredin.

Mae urddas mawr i mi
Ym mhob rhyw ffair a marchnad,
Ac uchel fydd fy mri
Ym mhlith pob gradd yn wastad,
Holl beudefigion byd
O'r bron sydd i'm croesawu ;
A'r tlodion braidd i gyd
Am danaf sy'n ymdynu.

Bydd Madog mynych-gwymp,
A'r Cegrwydd Mawr ab Torgest,
A'r Cloesgyn ar bob tymp,
I mi 'n ddilynwyr gonest :

Achubwr Cwpan Llawn,
A Gwargrwn ab tywalltgeg,
A fydd yn barchus iawn
O honof bob rhyw adeg.

Mae genyf lawer nod
I harddu fy minteioedd;
Yr wyf yn haeddu clod
O herwydd fy ngweithredoedd,
Bydd rhai a llygaid du,
Trwyn coch, a gweflau tewion,
A'r lleill o'm deiliaid cu
Dan gleisiau ac archollion.

Bydd dadwrdd ym mhob tŷ
Lle byddaf yn trigfanu,
A phawb yn ddigon hy
I alw ar ddiawl o'm deutu
A hyfryd genyf fi
Fydd gweled tori potiau,
A gwaed yn arferth li
Yn rhedeg hyd y lloriau.

Bydd clywed erchyll reg
Yn hyfryd gan fy nghalon

A phawb yn lledu ei geg
I ganu ffol bennillion;
A hoffus genyf fi
Fydd gweled dau gymydog
Yn ymladd fel dau gi,
Yn eithaf annrhugarog.

Mae pawb o dan y rhod
Yn meddu lle i orphwyso
Ir rhai fydd wedi bod
O danynt yu llafurio;
Gwayau bob dull
Sydd hefyd genyf finau
A mynueh iawn y cyll
Rhai ynddynt eu bywydau.

Bydd llawer yn y nos,
'Nol bod yn fy ngwas'naethu,
Yn gorwedd yn y ffos
Hyd nes bont wedi ffern
Bydd ereill hyd y ffyrdd,
A'r lleill yn y tomenau——
Mae genyf lwybrau fyrdd
I fyn'd i wineud angau.

Mi yrais Sion or Pant,
I orwedd ryw nos Wener,
Yn ymyl Ty'n y nat
Mewn eira hyd at ei hanner ;
Ca'dd yno oerfel blin,
Bu farw y'mhen ychydig.
Mae genyf fodd i drin
Fy neiliaid yn gythreutig.

Gorweddodd Sion o'r Cwm
Yn un o'm ben welyau
Nes fferu fel y plwm,
Pan oedd yn rhodio'r Gwyliau.
Mi dufiais ryw hen wr
F'un byw gerllaw i'r Rheidiol
I ganol llyn o ddwr
I foddi'n ddigon marwol.

A thaflais wr y Plas,
Yn ymyl afon Cunwy,
Oddiar ei gefyl glás,
I dori ei forddwyd aswy
A Dafis, gwr Ty mawr
Daflais dan ei gerbyd;
Bu'n gorwedd bedair awr
'Nol hyn yn methu symud.

Bu'm gyda Sion o'r Graig,
Nid pawb sy'n gwybod hyny,
Yn gorphen lladd ei wraig
Yr hon fu'n hir yn nychu;
A gyrais Wil Llwyn Glas
Iwànu ei gy mydog,
Ag erfyn yn ei gas——
Rwy'n hoffi pob dyn llidiog.

Mi wneuthum i cyn hyn
Nid ofnaf ddweud ar gyhoedd,
I Meistr Jones o'r Glyn
Ddifrodi ei dai a'i diroedd;
Bu'n cysgu lawer gwaith,
Y'n ol bod yn fy nghwmni,
Yn uganol chwech neu saith
O foch i Huw Sion Parri.

Bu gwr yr Hafod Lom
Gerllaw i Hendre'r Newyn,
Yn gorwedd yn y dom
Yn waetth ei drefn na mochyn,
Yr oedd ei wraig pryd hyn,
A'i blant yn wag ei boliau—
Nid pawb gaiff fara gwyn
Wrth rodio hyd fy llwybrau.

Mae'r brif-ffordd yn rhy gul
I rai o'm teulu cymmwys,
I fyned ar ddydd Sul
O'r capel ac o'r Eglwys,
O herwydd heibio i mi
Y galwant yn wastadol,
Heb feddwl mwy na'r ci
Fod ganddynt ran anfarwol

Aeth rhai o'm deiliaid i
Gymdeithas Cymedroldeb;
Pa ddrwg oedd hyn i mi,
Dim—haeraf yn eu hwyueb ;
Nid wyf yn hitiio draen
Yn y gymdeithas hono ;
Am fyned yn fy mlaen
Yr wyf,—pwy all fy rwystro.
W. EDWARDS.

Llanrwst, Argraffwyd gan John Jones.

---

and Abstinence: Observations on the Two Principles), printed by Hugh Hughes. It was published on a Saturday and the 500 copies had sold out by Monday morning, such was the intensity of interest in the subject and the reputation of the author and publisher in the Caernarfon area. The reprint was soon answered by a pamphlet from Morris Hughes of with

Can ddirwestol, sef Ymffrost Syr John Heidden, block by James Cope, c.1836-7.

CAN NEWYDD

AM LESHAD

DIR WEST.

Cenir ar "Belisle March."

Prydferthwch y Meddwyn.

YWAIN MEIRION.

Llanrwst, argraffwyd gan J. Jones.

Felinheli, followed by a further blast from Caledfryn and considerable comment from both sides published by Hughes in *Y Papyr Newydd Cymraeg*. In this atmosphere, the ballad singers also turned their attention to the subject. John Jones published two teetotal prints in the large format pictures by James Cope. Neither is dated, but they are probably from 1836 or 1837. The ballad *Ymffrost Syr John Heidden* (Sir John Barley-corn's Boast), written by Gwilym Padarn, is in traditional form. Syr John, who tells his own story, is a Welshified John Barleycorn, the embodiment of alcohol, and each verse suggests the unpleasant goings on associated with his influence. Some of the offences seem rather mild, and smack either of great puritanism or a distinct lack of commitment on the part of the writer:

Can Newydd am Leshad Dirwest, block by James Cope, c.1836-7.

> A hideous belch to hear
> My heart it so rejoices,
> Great gobs from ear to ear
> That shout their mindless verses....

Other verses identify more serious misdemeanours:

> By Sion o'r Graig I stood,
> This is a deadly secret,
> His wife all soaked in blood
> Long suff'ring pool of scarlet;
> I drove poor Wil in spite
> To thrash his next-door neighbour,
> Took pleasure in their fight,
> Egged on their evil labour...

Despite John Jones's advertisement of the sheet as a temperance ballad, John Barleycorn's subjects only reject his influence as far as the door of the Moderation Society. The ballad might predate the teetotal movement proper, which came to prominence about 1835, although the word was first used in England in 1833. We may presume that ballad singers, like most other people, took sides in this argument. James Cope's imagery is explicit and condemnatory. John Barleycorn is the Devil in not very convincing disguise. In the first picture his pitchfork is leant incon-spicuously against the wall, but in the second he reveals himself to carry off an inebriated gentleman in a striped waistcoat, Don Giovanni-like, to eternal hell-fire and damnation.

James Cope's picture ironically entitled *Prydferthwch y Meddwyn* (The Beauty of the Drunkard), printed with a ballad by Ywain Meirion, is among his finest. Staggering from the Anchor to the Cross Keys, a dissolute man advises his partner:

> 'Better late than never'
>   To leave
> Strong drink and indulgence:
> Don't touch the deadly poison
> Ever again, dear one.

The ballad is unambiguously teetotal. Listing the evil consequences of drink, which include wife beating, murder and suicide, resulting in poverty, hanging and transportation, Ywain Meirion assured his audience, presum-ably from personal experience, that moderation was not the answer:

> 'Tis better to Tee-total be,
> And keep your grip on life;
> Some people never can, we see,
> In moderation thrive...

The alcohol-free world was a paradise of marital bliss and prosperity:

> The drunks that once lived on these streets,
> Were all in tatters clad,
> But now they buy their fuel, their sheets,
> Their food 'gainst want, so glad;
> Now Doli in her finest gown,
> And Siani from Sir Fôn,
> Buy clothes for Ellis, coat and trousers
> All grand and new for Sion.

Given the social context in which the ballads were sung, it is difficult to

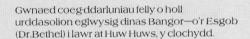

Gwnaed coeg-ddarluniau felly o holl urddasolion eglwysig dinas Bangor—o'r Esgob (Dr.Bethel) i lawr at Huw Huws, y clochydd.

Yr adeg hono yr oedd Nicander yn gurad yn yr Eglwys Gadeiriol, newydd ddychwelyd o Rydychain. Tynodd ŵg y *Figaro* drwy bregethu pregeth Buwseyaidd iawn o flaen un o gymdeithasau cyfeillgar y dref. Yr wythnos ganlynol ymddangosodd darlun o Mr Williams yn edrych oddiallan i ffenestr hen weithdŷ saer yn Llanystumdwy, ei ffedog o'i flaen, a llewys ei grys wedi eu torchi i fyny; gosodai ei fysedd yn rhês ar yr ermig mwyaf amlwg ar ei wyneb, a gwaeddai, 'Ffarwel—*Better Living!*' Yna, ceid darlun arall o hono yn ei wisgoedd offeiriadol yn pregethu 'Adenedigaeth yn Medydd', gyda'r *Cyffes Ffydd*, yr *Hyfforddwr*, a'r *Drysorfa* wedi eu lluchio yn ysgyrion ar hyd yr allor gerllaw.

Owen Owen Roberts, Bangor, by an unknown photographer, c.1860.

Figaro in Wales, block by Robert Roberts, 1835.

believe that there was not at least an element of send-up here, though the printed version may have found a market among the more zealous converts of all classes.

At the same time that Hugh Hughes, Caledfryn, and Josiah Thomas Jones were producing *Y Seren Ogleddol* in Caernarfon, Robert Jones was printing the English-language *Figaro in Wales*, a satirical monthly, in Bangor. Robert Jones was a grandson of Dafydd Jones, the Trefriw printer, and therefore a cousin to John Jones of Llanrwst. The *Figaro in Wales* was produced in association with Owen Owen Roberts of Bangor as editor and John Roberts of Holyhead. O.O. Roberts was a pioneer of public health and education in Caernarfon, Bangor and Llanrwst, a campaigning radical with a high profile. In 1832 he paid Lewis Evan Jones to reprint Evan Lloyd's poem *The Curate* in Caernarfon, indicating a sense of radical tradition among these nineteenth-century intellectuals extending back beyond Jac Glanygors. Aware that Lloyd was a priest, O.O. Roberts relished his precursor's attack on the hierarchy of the English church the more. The poem had included the lines:

> And he who ranks as *Knighthood's* glorious chief,
> Shares the high honour with a *loin of beef.*
> These gifts among the *mob of fortune* fall;
> One grain of honesty is worth them all—
> For Nature had decreed, that all should learn,
> Before they eat, their nourishment to earn.

The new edition included a brief but pointed foreword written by Roberts: "Published in the year 1766 but evidently intended for 1832."

O.O. Roberts would go on to attack the established church in two pamphlets of his own, published in 1834 and 1835, and to persuade the parishioners of Llanbeblig to refuse to pay their church rates in 1837.

The engraver John Roberts, like the printer of the *Figaro in Wales*, Robert Jones, had a good pedigree in the popular press, being the son of Robert Roberts, the printer of almanacks in Holyhead.[7] However, like most things connected with the *Figaro in Wales*, the details of his activities are obscure. The paper carried an attractive wood engraving on its title, showing the barber giving a respectable client, under protest, a very close shave, symbolising its attitude to the establishment generally. This was presumably the work of John Roberts. According to an account written within living memory of the publication of the paper by John Davies, Gwyneddon, it also issued cartoons. One was of Morris Williams, Nicander, a prominent high churchman, not long come down to Bangor from Oxford, heavily under the influence of Pusey.

"At that time, Nicander was a curate at the Cathedral... He drew the attention of the *Figaro* by preaching a very Puseyite sermon before one of the town's friendly societies. The following week appeared a picture of Mr Williams, looking out of an old carpenter's workshop in Llanystumdwy,[8] his apron around him and his shirt-sleeves rolled up; he cocks a snook as he shouts 'Farewell—Better Living!' Then there was another picture of him in his robes preaching 'Rebirth in Baptism', with the *Cyffes Ffydd*, the *Hyfforddwr*, and the *Trysorfa*, scattered like dry bones on the nearby altar."[9]

The cartoons have disappeared. They may have been issued on separate sheets or in one of the several issues of the paper of which no copy survives.

The *Figaro in Wales* soon got into legal difficulties. An Englishman, George Johnstone—"valiant poltroon" in the paper—failed to get in at the municipal election in Caernarfon in 1835, and took exception to his rough treatment by the *Figaro*. He sued the printer, Robert Jones. The case was heard at Bala where "The learned counsel read the article in which the alleged libel was contained, commenting on the various passages, some of which produced considerable laughter in court...." The judge, however, was not amused. "He said the motto of the paper—
    'I'll publish right or wrong,
    Fools are my theme, let satire be my song'
was worthy of the paper",[10] and under his direction the jury awarded a massive £250 damages. Flushed by success, Johnstone next sued L.E. Jones of Caernarfon for selling the paper, and pocketed another £100. Needless to say, the *Figaro in Wales* was closed down.

In his essay in 1884, Gwyneddon described a second cartoon (or, possibly, series of cartoons) published in the *Figaro*:

"So cartoons were drawn of all of Bangor's church dignitaries—from the Bishop (Dr. Bethel) down to Huws, the bell-ringer."

If the writer was correct in associating this cartoon with the *Figaro*, then it has disappeared, like those of Nicander. However, it seems more likely that Gwyneddon was recording a muddled recollection of a cartoon published with a ballad against the Bishop by L.E. Jones in Caernarfon at the end of 1841. The date, location and style of the cartoon make it most likely to be the work of James Cope. The occasion was the celebration organised with the support of the Bishop on the baptism of Arthur, first son of Victoria and Albert, made Prince of Wales on 8 December.

Reactions in the popular press to this event, and to royal occasions in general, were distinctly mixed. As we have seen, Hugh Hughes had produced wood engravings for *Y Cymro* of both the deceased (and generally popular) George IV and of the new King William IV and Queen Adelaide in 1830 and 1831, to accompany loyal texts. In Cardigan, Isaac Thomas also published royal portraits, although on the only surviving example Princess Victoria has become Mary Morris of Radnorshire whose mother drowned herself "in malice" on her marriage to one John Jones. Windsor Castle is in the background. Isaac Thomas celebrated the marriage of Victoria and Albert in 1840 with a picture and a loyal address by Joseph Hughes, Carn Ingli, an expatriate poet originally from Newport, Pembrokeshire. Like the other two, Isaac Thomas's print of the baptism in

January 1842 is almost certainly based on a London original.

However, in London the event also sparked the rather more cynical mind of the cartoonist C.J. Grant into action. *The Grand Procession in honour of the arrival of the Prince of Wales* revived Poor Taff on his goat, after a long period of sleep, complete with toasted cheese and leek, but added new elements to the stereotype almost exactly two hundred years after its debut in the popular prints. The Bard, on loan from high art, made a rare appearance at the other end of the market, but the most important innovation was the dancing milkmaids in tall black hats. The efforts of Augusta Hall, Lady Llanofer, to codify the remnants of medieval dress, surviving in Wales, into a national costume, were given a high profile at the Abergavenny Eisteddfodau in the 1830s.[11] The flannel skirt, shawl and especially the tall beaver hat, provided an instantly recognisable token of nationhood, not available to Thomas Pennant to identify his Mother Cambria in 1785. Grant's image was transitional—one of the few occasions when Poor Taff would keep company with the female stereotype of Welshness which swept him away for ever in mid-century. The text, which mocks the loyalty of the Welsh to this pompous parody of nationhood, is also a combination of the throw-back and the innovative:

"The auspicious (suspicious) Event, as joyous, as honourable and glorious, to JOHN BULL and his brother TAFFY, was SILLY-brated by the latter (at the great expense of the former), by a grand Triumphal Entry of his Royal Highness (whom BOB preserve,) into his loving and loyal Principality. ORDER OF THE PROCESSION: A body of Cornish Navigators, with Shovels and Pickaxes to clear the way (not seen, as unfit, owing to their being joyfully drunk, at the circumstance of his Royal Highness being also Duke of Cornwall); A Milkman bearing a Banner, upon which are emblazon'd his Highness's Arms and Motto. 2. Anxcient Welsh Harpers playing and singing an old Royal Song, call'd 'Werry like a Whale.' A Superb MILK-CAN, drawn by six CREAM-coloured Nannies, containing his Royal Highness, invested with his Robes, Cap and Feathers, &c., follow'd by the chief members of the oldest families in Walliae (all those who can trace their pedigree in an uninterrupted line from Adam's great grandfather). After the Cheese Bearers comes a number of handsome Milk-maids, dancing to the tune of 'JENNY JONES,' with Pails full of CURDS AND WHEY to give AWAY to Children; (HEIRS to Welsh WHIGS only.) The Procession is closed by his Royal Highness's Body Guards, the Billy Brigade, (invulnerable in Mountain Warfare.)"

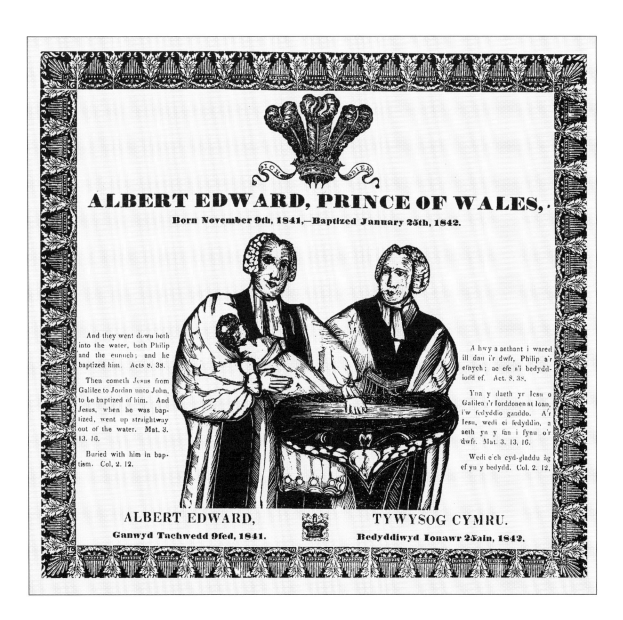

ALBERT EDWARD, PRINCE OF WALES,

Born November 9th, 1841,—Baptized January 25th, 1842.

And they went down both into the water, both Philip and the eunuch; and he baptized him. Acts 8. 38.

Then cometh Jesus from Galilee to Jordan unto John, to be baptized of him. And Jesus, when he was baptized, went up straightway out of the water. Mat. 3. 13. 16.

Buried with him in baptism. Col. 2. 12.

A hwy a aethant i wared ill dau i'r dwfr, Philip a'r eunuch; ac efe a'i bedyddiodd ef. Act. 8. 38.

Yna y daeth yr Iesu o Galilea i'r Iorddonen at Ioan, i'w fedyddio ganddo. A'r Iesu, wedi ei fedyddio, a aeth yn y fan i fynu o'r dwfr. Mat. 3. 13, 16.

Wedi e'ch cyd-gladdu âg ef yn y bedydd. Col. 2. 12.

ALBERT EDWARD,

Ganwyd Tachwedd 9fed, 1841.

TYWYSOG CYMRU.

Bedyddiwyd Ionawr 25ain, 1842.

131

The conventional wisdom in the period that Welsh milk sellers, who were prominent in the trade in London, habitually watered down their product—that Taffy was still a thief—was emphasised in Grant's other cartoon on the theme, *Baptism of the Prince of the Taffies*, published in *The Penny Satirist*. A water pump disgorges into the milk can among the Welsh contingent, who are joined by Prince Albert's compatriots satirised as sausages and broom girls. Between them, "Old Mammy Church, the State Dairy-keeper and Royal udder squeezer [is] in the act of pouring the contents of the *Jordan* upon the sensorium of his Royal Papship." Mammy Church is strangely prescient of Dame Wales, half a century later, though it seems unlikely that J.M. Staniforth would have seen this isolated earlier embodiment of his creation.

James Cope's satire on the occasion of the baptism of Prince Arthur was more complex, and not aimed directly at royalty but at Toryism in general and the English church in particular. The Tory newspaper, *The North Wales Chronicle*, known to radicals as "Papyr Bangor" and "Y Palas Gazette" (that is, the Bishop's palace in Bangor, not the Queen's palace in London), was implicated for having printed the handbills advertising the celebrations, along with the Bishop himself who had contributed £20. The satire is distinctly puritanical in tone, criticising the revival of the kind of Sunday games and sports—mule races, catching a pig with a soaped tail, climbing the greasy pole—which Methodists, in particular, had done much to stamp out fifty years before.

> Each lousy lubber, lazy lout,
> 　Come forward, brave and fine,
> With rogues and robbers, grubby whelps,
> 　Cain's family to join.
>
> All Sabbath sinners, donkey owners
> 　Let one and all consort;
> The English Moors, Belphegor's whores,
> 　Will sponsor mindless sport.
>
> Some vapid vicars, fatuous fiddlers,
> 　are smiling at the pitch;
> While *parchus* gents of the church descend
> 　like blind men to the ditch.

The eighteenth-century world of Evan Lloyd—the world of satire and popular prints—had been turned upside down. The dour and puritanical

Baptism of the Prince of the Taffies, by C.J. Grant, 1842.

No credit due, by J.M.Staniforth, 1908.

Pob lluman lleuog, pob llabi diog,
    Yn wrol de'wch yn mlaen,
I w—a lladron, a ch'nawon budron,
    Mae gwa'dd gan deulu Cain.

Pob torwr Sul, pob perchen Mul,
    Na fydded un yn ol;
Mae Eglwys Loegr, merch Belffegor,
    Am noddi campiau ffol.

Bydd rhai Ficeriaid, ffol Ffidleriaid,
    Yn gwenu ar y gwaith;
A pharchedig Wyr Eglwysig
    Fel deillion ar eu taith.

Nonconformists he had detested had acquired a satirical sense of humour and learned to use the vulgar media of the people to press home their attack on the Church of England and the irreligious, pre-revival way of life it still represented in their minds. Radicalism and licentiousness had been separated by the new breed in Wales who promoted progress and sobriety as necessary bedfellows.

    Come see a Bishop, black as night
        Like Jehu on his mule;
    And greasy priests, devoid of grace,
        And narrow curate fools.

    They groaned and swore as they chased the boar,
        They cursed his slippery tail;
    And some would spit and some would s–t,
        Like pigs beyond the pale.

The cartoon has Belphegor in clerical bands presiding over the Bishop and his clergy at their sport, in front of the cathedral. In the background, on the other side of the fence, one of the populace holds a placard with the slogan "Down with Nonconformism. The Church for Ever!" Two ballads accompany the picture, both anonymous since they certainly libel the Bishop, his church and his National School. They are most unlikely to be the work of a ballad singer but might have come from any one of the radical group of O.O. Roberts, Caledfryn and Hugh Hughes:

    Who would sell their freedom and chain themselves so tight,
    To hear a donkey's Amen, a mule's inane insight?
    They hoard their bitter tithes and offerings of all kinds,
    Not God's but Mammon's order, the law that fills their minds.

Gwahoddiad i Adferiad Gwylmabsant Bangor, by James Cope, 1841, over page.

133

GWAHODDIAD
I ADFERIAD GWYLMABSANT BANGOR.

YR HWN A GYFHELIR

Gyda Races Mulod, Hela Moch, ac amrywiol Grist'nogol Gampau, o dan nodded
Uchel Offeiriadau yn nyddiau Nadolig, Blwyddyn yr Arglwydd 1841.*

GWAHODDIAD.

Pob lluman lleuog, pob llabi diog,
Yn wrol de'wch yn mlaen,
I w——— a lladron, a ch'nawon budron,
Mae gwa'dd gan deulu Cain.

Pob torwr Sul, pob perchen Mul,
Na fydded un yn ol;
Mae Eglwys Loegr, merch Belffegor,
Am noddi campiau ffol.

Bydd rhai Ficeriaid, ffol Ffidleriaid,
Yn gwênu ar y gwaith;
A pharchedig Wŷr Eglwysig
Fel deillion ar eu taith.

Yn lle Gair Duw, i ddynol ryw,
A 'Fengyl i rai gwael,
Mae gan Olynion, yr Apostolion
Ryw gampdlws ffol i'w gael.

I weled golwg mor ddihalog
Dan nodded urddol wyr,
Doed pob meddwyn, a phob oferddyn,
A lleban drwg ei lun.

O mor hynod! Races Mulod!
O fewn Esgobawl dre'!
Pan bydd bagad o drueiniaid
Yn ll'wgu yn y lle!

Cael gweled Esgob, du ei sipog,
Fel Jehu ar ei Ful;
Offeiriad bras, heb arwydd gras,
Ac ambell Gurad cul.

A hen Eglwyswyr, ffug anlladwyr,
Yn bodio Nani noeth
Pan yn ei chrys, yn fawr ei chwys,
'Rol enill bara poeth.

Gwel'd rhai yn dringo, ac yn gwingo,
Hyd Bolyn am Gap Ffwl;
A'r lleill yn grinio am eu cinio,
Fel monkies ar glostwl.

Bydd rhai yn tuchan wrth Hela Mochyn,
Dan regi ei gynffon lefn;
A rhai mewn sacha, wedi c———a,
Yn waeth na moch eu trefn.

Bydd Hunter Brown, wrth chwareu'r Clown
A newyn yn y wlad,
Yn ddrwg ei ddull, hen hangmon byll,
Yn rhefru Bara Rhad.

A llawer Suddas, gyda malais,
Am dreisio a gwasgu'r gwan;
Rhai llyfn eu gwyneb, llawn glythineb,
Gwir babaidd wŷr y Llan.

Bydd amryw rigwm o ———u y degwm
Gan Uchel Wŷr y Llan,
Ac yn ei gader, ar ol eu pader,
Y D——l yn dyweyd, Amen.

GWYLMABSANT BANGOR.

YSMALA'N Ras y Mulod, oedd canfod Esgob call,
A llu o Offeiriadau, i gyd fel dynion dall;
Parchedig Wyr y Coleg, yn troi i redeg Ras,
Ac Esgob ar gefn Asyn yn debyg i greyr glas.

A phob rhyw foliog Berson a'i drwyn wrth gynffon Mul,
Mwy hyddyag ar y chwareu, na'r Salmau ar y Sul;
A'r wenwisg deg am dano, yn chwifio yn y gwynt
A'i berwig yn ei ddilyn, yn ail i Gilpin gynt.

A phawb trwy hyn yn profi, fel Pusey'n chwareu pel,
Olyniaeth Apostolaidd, yn ngrym eu santaidd sel,
Fel Doctor Hook, a Newman, n'r truan Oxford Tracts
Yn profi nad yw'r 'Senters, a'r Quakers ddim ond Quacks.

A thwyllo felly'r tlodion, a'u dwyn fel Samson gynt
I chwareu i'r Philistiaid, i'w gweled yn y gwynt,
Prinhau yn gul yr epha, a chodi'r bara'n bell
O gyrhaedd yr anghenus, heb geiniog yn ei gell.

A rhai yn rhwym mewn sachau, a'u coesau fel mewn cas,
Rhai a eu trwynau'n syrthio, wrth risio yn y Ras,
Hen wragedd blin yn rhegi, a phlant yn gweiddi gair,
Difyrwch i Bersoniaid, fel ffyliaid yn y ffair.

Gwirioni hen wrageddos â choces ac â chig,
A'r rhai fo'n colli'r campio, yn d——lio yn eu dig;
Ac am yr ucha neidio a dawnsio am bwys o de,——
Personiaid yna'n bloeddio yn roario oll——Hwre!

Maent wedi gallu llwyddo, i dwyllo llawer dyn,
En bod yn caru'r tlodion, 'ai llymion gwael eu llun,
Rhoi amryw elusenau, r wn twyll yn nrysau eu tai,
Ond hyn ni wna anghen——rai llymion ronyn llai.

Nid ydyw eu holl ragrith, ond melldith yn mhob man,
A rhyw beth i ddal tlodion, rai noethion, byth yn wan,
Neu fel rhoi rhyw friwsionyn, i gi wrth gadwyn yw,
Rhyw damaid rhag eu ll'wgu i'w cadw i fyny'n fyw.

Pe byddent yn dymuno, eu helpio hwy a'u hil,
Hwy dorent eu cadwynau, n fan fan ddarnau fil,
A dygent wyr yr angen, uwchlaw elusen lwyd,
Nes byddent drwy eu dyddiau, heb eisiau gwaith na bwyd.

Mae'n hawdd i Berson bawlyd, cybyddlyd yn y bon,
Gael parch gan ddynion lledffol, wrth ffugio duwiol dân,
Os rhydd o iddynt arian, dan lolian o ryw lun,
Er na bo dimau'n dyfod, o'i hynod bwrs ei hun.

Rhai erchyll yw'r Personiaid plynyid yr hen Lane,
Y maent o duedd aflen, y gigfran 'ran eu gwane,
Eu perfedd a orlwythant, a drewant yn ddidrefn,
Ac wedi meddwi, llyncu, gwnaent chwydu'r drwyel
drachefn.

Ysbio drwy y Golar, a fydd yr arfer nice,
A'r hwn edrycho hylla, mi a'i profa, geiff y prize,
Gwynebau mewn gwan obaith, rai diffaeth fel y d——l,
Fel hyn y gwerthfawr brizes, yn hwylus ddaw i'w hawl.

A'r pen Policeman 'Sgobol, an'styriol hefo ei staff,
A'r p'lice sy dan ei aden, ro'nt lawer hearty laugh;
Caiff Mochyn ei seboni, a'i lyfnu gyda'i law,
A rhedir ar ol hwnw, mewn berw, chwys, a baw.

Rhed Merched yn eu crysau, a'u gwalltiau yn y gwynt,
Am wel'd y sport hyfrydion, rhydd Person lawer punt;
Mawr fydd y floedd a'r chwerthin, wrth lyncu'r pwdin
poeth.
A dringo'r polyn ired, er niwed i'r d——n noeth.

O bobpeth ga'dd ei lunio, i geisio twyllo'r gwan,
Hwn yma yw'r ffieidd-dra, atgasaf fu'n un man;
Râs Mulod yn lle Bara i dori eisiau dyn!
Ffei honynt! P'le mae teimlad offeiriad anhoff un?

Ai codi'n ol o'r domen, arferion yr hen Fall,
Sy'n brawf fod ganddynt grefydd, a ffydd yr hon ni phall?
Ai llygru'r byd sy'n gweddu i'r Clergy mawr eu clod?
A fydd y Lloi melynion, yn Bethel† eto'n bod?

Beth nesaf a ddyfeisir gan deulu Pusey'r pen?
Ai'r "Book of Sports"‡ i ddarllenir, gan wŷr yr anwiog
wen?
A fydd i'r holl Blwyfolion, a'r Person chwareu pel,
Ar dalcen yr hen glochdai, y Suliau mewn mawr sel?

Y maent yn dysgu'r ie'nctyd, yn hyfryd yn ein hoes,
I barchu'r offeren-grys——i gredu'r hen gi's groes——
Dweyd celwydd yw'r peth cynta' wna'u caticismau cas,
Sef fod ar annuwiolion, arwyddion o wir râs.

Rhyw Nationalaidd flinder, ysgeler yw eu School——
Ni chânt i'w chadw'n unman ond dynan fyddo'n ddwi,
Neu benbwl haner gwirion, sy'n foddlon i ryw fyd;
Gwel pawb ond, rhai rhy ddylion, drwy gastiau hon i gyd.

Pwy byth a wertha'i ryddid, i fyn'd i did mor den,
I wrando breñad asyn, a mul yn dweyd Amen?
Caru y maent y degwm, a'r offrwm o bob rhyw,
A phorthi cnawdol chwantau, yn fwy na deddfau Duw.

* Cynhaliwyd Cyfarfod yn National School Room, Bangor, ar ddydd Iau, y 9fed o'r mis presenol (Rhagfyr) i benderfynu y modd mwyaf addas i orfoleddu am Enedigaeth Tywysog Cymru. Y Cadeirydd oedd y Parchedig John Hamer, M.A. Casglwyd swm o arian, oddeutu 70 punt yn y cyfarfod hwnw, ac wedi hyny, ar hyd y dref o dŷ i dŷ, oddeutu 50 pnnt yn rhagor. Hysbyswyd ar ol hyn, drwy Handbills, wedi eu printio gan John Brown, perchenog Papyr Bangor, yr hwn a elwir yn gyffredin, "y Pala Gazette," o herwydd ei fod o dan arolygiad yr Uchel Bersoniaid, y byddai cyfarfod ar Ddydd Calan, sef y 1af o Iouawr, 1842, yn y National School, i gyfranu i'r Tylodion Wrthbanau, &c. &c. am ddeg o'r gloch; ac am un o'r gloch i Hela Mochyn wedi seboni ei gynffon; i redeg Mulod; dringo hyd Bolyn; neidio mewn Sachau; smocio am y goreu, &c. &c. Yn mhlith cynorthwywyr ereill i'r gwaith, ymddengys enw'r Arglwydd Esgob am ugain punt; y Gwir Barchedig y Deon am dair punt; y Parchedig J. Hamer am ddwy bunt; a'r Parchedig H. Price am ddwy bunt.

† 1 Bren. xii. 28.

‡ Y " Book of Sports" ydoedd lyfr, yn cynwys pob math o ynfyd gampau a ffol ddigrifwch, a fyddai'r Offeiriaid yn ddarllen wrth yr allor, fel rhan o wasanaeth yr Eglwys yn amser Charles yr Ail. Oddiar y fath halogrwydd y tarddodd yr amdreigliad Diwygiol, yr hon yw bost pob gwir Brotestant, ond yr hon y mae yr Oxford Tracts a Phapistiaid Eglwys Loegr, yn y dyddiau presenol, yn ei melldithio fel yn hollol groes i'r peth y maent hwy yn ei galw yr Eglwys Lân Catholic. Yn nheyrnasiad Charles yr Ail y gosodwyd Treth gyntaf ar Yd Tramor. Mae Treth yr Yd yn felldith drom ar y deyrnas yn y dyddiau presenol. Gobeithiwn na bydd i ail argraffiad o'r "Book of Sports," gael ei arferyd gan yr Offeiriadau yn nghyda Llyfr y Weddi Gyffredin yn y Llanau, ac fel llaw-lyfr plant yn y National Schools.

L. E. JONES, ARGRAFFYDD, HEOL Y BONT, CAERNARFON.

The attack of the Chartists on the Westgate Hotel, Newport, Nov. 4th 1839

The English Church was by far the most common target for criticism and satire by radical intellectuals in the first half of the nineteenth century. It was, by then, a safe target, no longer likely to lead to accusations from England of sedition, since Church abuses were much criticised in that country also. This was important in view of the continuing hyper-sensitivity of most Welsh intellectuals to criticism from the English. Indeed, attacks on Anglo-Catholicism and Puseyism could be made to seem a defence of the true British protestant tradition, sublimating particularly Welsh resentments and frustrations. Intellectuals were constrained, as ever, by their sense of history, at the centre of which was their proprietorial feeling of Britishness and, in consequence, their grotesquely exaggerated loyalty.

Nonconformism further constrained the expression of their politics. Conservatives, like John Elias, while recognising the existence of abuses, took the view that the established order was a consequence of God's providence, and that rejection of it was perilously close to a rejection of God.[12] Radicals like Hugh Hughes believed that God's greatest gifts to mankind were freedom of conscience and a rational intellect. This, and God's essential benevolence, meant that it was surely his intention that reason—and reason alone—was the means to change. Violent agitation against injustice was anathema to both groups. These factors may well account for the lack of visualisation in the popular press of civil disturbance in Wales in the years 1831-1843. The lack is striking, because those years were both the most disturbed since the Civil War, and coincided with the emergence of visual images in the popular press for the first time on a substantial scale.

The Merthyr Rising of 1831, the Chartist agitation culminating in the armed attack on the authorities at Newport in 1839, and the Rebecca Riots of 1839-1843, produced a meagre crop of ballads, pamphlets and printed images made in Wales itself. The Newport rising, as we have seen, was condemned by Ywain Meirion but was recorded and published as a lithograph by the artisan painter James Flewitt Mullock. He had been born in the town in 1818, and so was a young man when the rising took place. His attitude to the events depicted is unclear. Mullock was certainly a

The attack of the Chartists on the Westgate Hotel, Newport, Nov. 4th 1839, by James Flewitt Mullock, c.1840.

135

The Attack on the Westgate Hotel, engraved by W. Clerk after W. Howell, c. 1840.

The Welch Chartist Martyrs, engraved by W. Clerk, c. 1840.

progressive and would become a prominent figure in the development of civic amenities of various sorts in Newport over a long period. However, the image does not seem to over-dramatise the events. Indeed, the crowd in front of the Westgate Hotel is smaller than that depicted in a second print, signed by W. Howell and copied on stone by W. Clerk for a London publisher. A third, more dramatic rendition, certainly derived from these prints appeared in a book published in Newport the year after the event, *The Rise and Fall of Chartism in Monmouthshire*. In the same volume, a woodcut of the three leaders, Zephaniah Williams, John Frost and William Jones, came closest to presenting the persons involved in a heroic light. The images of these three were published as a separate sheet, lithographed by the same W. Clerk, over the sombre text of the judge's death sentence, subsequently commuted.[13]

The negative reaction of Ywain Meirion to the uprising may reflect an unwillingness on the part of many rural people, as well as of the inhabitants of the older towns, to identify themselves with the new and cosmopolitan industrial communities. However, the attitude that the riots were an aberration, foreign to Welshness and inspired by outsiders, was more commonly expressed by intellectuals on their behalf. The contemporary disturbances in rural Carmarthenshire and Pembrokeshire were more difficult to dismiss in this way. First turnpike gates were broken down but eventually workhouses were also attacked under the leadership of the mysterious Beca. Nonetheless, Hugh Hughes attempted, in 1848, to condemn the disturbances as the work of irreligious outsiders. Sedition was an English phenomenon:

"In the year 1843, what was called the 'Rebecca' riots commenced in South Wales, and in 1839 the Chartist outrage occurred in Monmouthshire. Both originated with, and were conducted by men, not of the unenfranchised, and *unanglified* Welsh, but chiefly by Englishmen. The

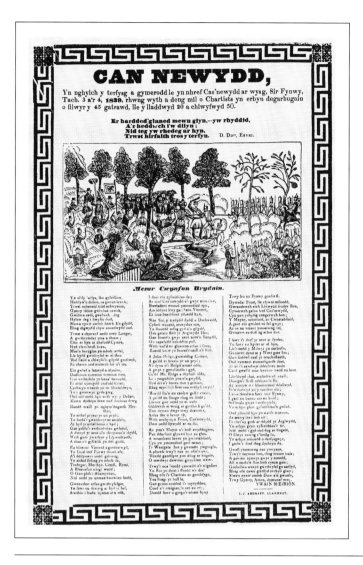

working classes of Wales were not the parties principally aggrieved by the *turnpike* impositions; and as to Chartism, the Welsh, unacquainted with the English language, had known nothing of its principles, but had lived entirely beyond the pale of its influence. Dissenters in particular, of every grade, were not only uncontaminated with English infidelity and insubordination, but they were the chief impediments in the way of the success of both the riotous movements alluded to..."[14]

As in the case of the exotic borrowed woodcut used to illustrate Ywain Meirion's ballad on the Chartists by John Jones, no one ventured to produce an image which projected Beca as a popular heroine (or hero), thereby providing a visual focus for the expression of support for the movement. Levi Gibbon's ballad on the disturbances certainly takes a more positive view than Ywain Meirion's earlier effort, but begins with the poet cautiously distancing himself from any direct acquaintance with those involved, and making light of the politics of the matter by a generally bawdy tone:

> I must tell you all at the start of my song,
> That I'm saying no slander nor blaming for wrong;
> There is an old woman who's still in this world,
> Though I've never heard her, nor seen her hair curled.
>
> Her name it is Beca, I'll tell you no lies,
> There's no woman like her for men in her thighs;
> She's worse than a rabbit for breeding, they say,
> With six hundred children and more every day...

The ironic ballad proceeds to describe the narrow escape of two activists. It was clearly written about 1842, before the riots reached their peak and before the leaders were arrested and transported:

Can Newydd, Yn nghylch y terfysg a gymerodd le yn nhref Cas'newydd..., published by John Jones, Llanrwst, c. 1839-40.

137

Hanes Bywyd Becca a'i Merched, published by Isaac Thomas, Cardigan, c.1842.

They promised men money for telling a tale,
But Beca continues to rob and to flail;
Merchant, the bastard, got a hundred gold pounds'
For 'cusing and lying without any grounds.

In English much better than mine he did bleat,
But Beca will trample him under her feet;
Two men from this country were dragged into gaol,
For that dirty pig and his mischievous tale.

Innocent, blameless, and upright and loyal,
No thieving with Beca was proved at their trial;
The law called them innocent, honest and free,
That truth is a virtue we all can agree.

They came from the prison both high in esteem,
And now they're at home as they always had been;
Though quartered like thieves under law's lock and key,
Today they are talking and laughing with glee.

With no fear of soldier nor lawyer nor law,
Proud Beca rides on, her white horse to the fore;
No matter how great is our Beca's attack,
There's no one knows anything, no tongue is slack...

The ballad is more of an exercise in the creation of an outlaw folk hero like Ned Kelly than in stirring up political discontent. It's all a bit of a lark. To accompany Levi Gibbon's ballad Isaac Thomas, perhaps constrained as much by the limited inventiveness of his engraver as by political caution, offered an elaborately dressed gentleman with a sword, surrounded by tropical vegetation, as the militia, hailed by one of his several Amazonian ladies standing in for Beca. It was left to the English press to provide the special pictures. The origin of the most romantic of these Becas, mounted and in exotic dress, is obscure, but the newly established *Illustrated London News* kept a close eye on events. Their report, which accompanied a picture entitled *The Welsh Rioters*, was condemnatory, but a second and more sympathetic piece, written later in 1843, hinted at both the legitimacy of the cause and the myth-making potential of the remedy:

"Rebecca has now been allowed almost time to grow into a heroine—she is the leader of hundreds of men, and instead of confining her crusade to turnpikes, she has turned her forces to the besiegal of workhouses—defying magistrates and constables as contemptuously as she did erst the guardians of the toll—and pursuing her labour of demolition with a recklessness quite in keeping with the whole spirit and romance of the mischievous adventure in which she and her followers have been engaged."[15]

The paper dispatched an artist in order to present to its readers "a series of engravings of what are but too truly termed 'the disturbed districts' of this interesting country." The result was a rather tame series of views of people and places, and only one further imaginative attempt to visualise Beca herself.

Like the literature of Dic Penderyn, hanged for his part in the Merthyr rising, the most memorable record of the Rebeca riots was a ballad of personal tragedy, *Hiraeth David Davies, Dai Cantwr, pan yn Garcharor yn Nghaerfyrddin, am y terfysg yn Amser Rebeca* (The Lament of David Davies, Dai Cantwr, when a Prisoner in Carmarthen for the riots in the Times of Rebeca). It was written when he and Sioni 'Sgubor Fawr—recorded at the same time by the artisan painter John Cambrian Rowland—were awaiting transportation to Australia. Some of the many printed versions were accompanied by conventional but appropriate woodcuts of a sailing ship:

I am become a shadow in the world,
Forsaken, my inheritance lost,
Wounded by the heavy blow,
That has fallen upon me
In my youth, evil is my share;

CAN NEWYDD;
Sef, Hanes Bywyd Becca a'i Merched.

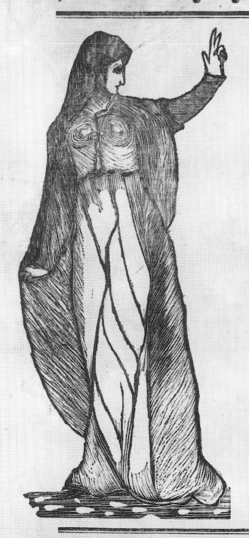

1 HOLL fechgyn a merched, trwy'r ardal o'r bron,
'Rwy'n galw pob oedran, o bob man, yn llon;
Y tlawd a'r cyfoethog, yn serchog eich gran,
Dewch yma gael clywed rhyw hanes ar gân.

2 Wrth ddechren llefaru 'rwy'n gwaeddi ar go'dd,
Nid wyf yn enllibio, na beio'n un modd;
Ond coffa rhiw fenyw sydd heddyw mewn bod,
Nid wyf wedi'i chlywed, na'i gweled erio'd.

3 Ei henw yw Becca, mi wealdda'n dra hy,
'Does yma un fenyw am wrxw fel hi;
Mae'n waeth na chwn'n zen i esgor ar blant,
Mae ganddi o ferched, 'rwy'n clywed, chwech cant.

4 Ac, etto, mae'n esgor ar ragor o hyd,
Os par hi fel yna hi tanwa'r holl fyd;
Van clo'rhên famaeth heb ddant yn ei gên,
Bydd Becca'r pryd hyny gael Baby'n rhy hên.

5 E, c'uifer o ferched a ddygodd i'r byd,
Mae Becca, hyd heddyw, yn weddw o hyd;
'Does shaith cydymaith i'r eneth, 'rwy'n siwr,
Mae Becca'n cenedin mewn gwaiy heb wr.

6 Mi glywais am Becca, mi fentra', gan' waith,
I rioed am ei phtiod ni chlywais un waith;
Mae Becca a'i merched fel gwilied trwy'r wlad,
Wel, d'wedwch, os gellwch, Pwy ydyw eu tad.

7 'Rwy'n crynu, ar droion, rhag ofon ei chwrdd,
Beth sydw hi'n hidlo fy nghornio fel hwrdd;
Ond, etto, 'rwy'n deall fod Becca mor gall,
Na chlymmer hi gant-punt am flino dyn dall.

8 Ca'dd Becca ei geni yn nghymru, fel fi,
Yn talan corfforol, yn mhlwyf Manachlogddu;
Fe dyfodd i fyno yn uchel ei phen,
Fe gym'rodd lawn feddiant o Gate'r Efel wen.

9 Bu yno fel Lady'n teyrnasu am dra,
Fe wua..th i'r cwnstabli garlamu ar ffo;

Fe dorodd y toll-borth yn gandryll i'r llawr,
Fel gallom, heb dalu, gael tramwy'r ffordd fawr.

10 Mae llawer yn gwaeddi, a hyny wrth chwant,
O rigion eu bola, 'da Becca a'i phlant;
'Rwyf finnau, fel baby, yn crynu, mewn cro'n,
Heb ganmol na chablu, rwy'n tewi a son.

11 Mae'n well genyf drenlio diwrnod neu ddau,
Heb brofi tobaco na smoco na chnau,
A gwasgu fy mola, mi waedda'n dra hy,
Na chlywed fod Becca am ymladd â mi.

12 Mae Becca 'rwy'n sicr o nattur mor frwd,
Pe bawn yn ei digio gwnai siglo fy nghwd;
Mi e n blino'r gwyr mawrion ar droion yn drwm,
Hi all pe bai'n leiciu sibedo dyn llwm.

13 Er maint yw'r bugeilia sy ar Becca a'i phlant,
Mae'n myned a'i llwybr, mae'n eglur, wrth chwant;
Hi dorrodd y toll-byrth wrth heol Llwyndu,
Do, dair gwaith neu bedair, hen leider yw hi.

14 Ba yno gwnstabli, ac hefyd bolis,
A llawer o soldiers mewn pwer am fis,
Er rhwystr i Becca ledratta'r ben glwyd,
Fel caffo pob gateman bryd cyfan o fwyd,

15 Mae arfau rhyfela gan Becca'n barhaus,
Ca'dd llawer eu clwyfo wrth waitio'r ben bais;
Bu rhywun yn rhywle dan ddannau'r llif draws,
Wel, gartre mi safaf heb fara na chaws.

16 Mae Becca a'i mherched mor ffalsed a'r ffox,
Mae'n torri rhai clwydi mor fân a phren clox;
Pan fyddo bugeiliaid yn gwylied man draw,
Mae Becca man obry yn totri'u ddifraw.

17 Mae Becca a'u thenlu yn saethu rip rap,
Gwnaeth goiled o friwid o dollborth P'llltrap;
Ac hefyd Trefechan fy hunan sydd dyst,
Wel, 'nawr mi ofyna, ai Becca yw'r Trust?

Er addo gwobrwyon i ddynion am ddweud,
Parhau i ledratta mae Becca yn wneud;
Daeth Merchant y mochyn i 'mofyn cann punt,
Am haeru celwyddau heb cisian'r fath hynt,

19 Mae hwnw mewn british mwy mentris na fi,
Gall Becca pan gwrddo ei droedio fel ei;
Aeth dau o'r cym'dogaeth yn 'sgyfaith i'r jail
O achos 'rhen fochwr a'i ddwndwr disail.

20 'Roedd rheiny'n wastadol yn hollol ddifrad,
Heb ddysgu lledratta 'da Becca a'i hâd;
Fe chwariodd y cyfraith yn odiaeth o'u plaid,
Fe saif y gwitionedd mewn rhinwedd wrth raid.

21 Daeth rhei'ny o'r carchar, mewn ffafar a chlod,
Maent 'nawr yn cartref, mor llon ag erio'd;
Er llechu dan gloeion, fel lladron, am dro,
Maent heddyw, 'rwy'n credu, yn canu di do,

22 'Does ofon gwasanaeth, na chyfraith, na dim,
Mae Becca'n ben uchel ar gefen cel gwru;
Er maint yw'r lledrata wnaeth Becca a'i rhyw,
'Does undyn, er synded, yn gwybod pwy'n yw.

23 Mae Becca fel bwci'n gweithredu 'rhyd nôs,
Bydd llawer yn chwerthyn wel'd terfyn ei ho's;
Hi aeth a'i cheneddaeth i Azbeth mewn grym,
Fe dynodd y caerau a'r yctau i'r dim.

24 Holl hanes Rebecca, mi waedda'n dra hy,
Nis gallaf ei gofio, na'i goffa i chwi;
Yn nghymru a lloeger mae llawer oswai,
O achos fod Becca'n lledrata fel mae.

25 Yn awr 'rwy'n terfynu fy ffwdan a'm ffair,
Mi garwn wel'd heddwch, os coeliwch fy ngair;
Boed llwyd'llaut yn wastad, i gariad, heb sen,
Fod rhyngom â Becca, mi waedda Amen,

LEVI GIBBON, Cwmfelin, a'i cânt.

Drych i fyd wyf i fod,
Collais glod all'swn gael,
Tost yw'r nod, dyrnod wael,
  I'w gafael ddaeth â mi,
Yn fy ie'nctid drygfyd ddaeth,
Yn lle rhyddid, caethfyd
  maith
  'Chwanegwyd er fy ngofid,
Alltud wyf ar ddechra'm taith,
  Ca'm danfon o fy ngwlad,
Ty fy nhad, er codiad tirion,
  I blith y duon gor,
Dros y môr o'm goror gron,
O'r fath ddrygyn i mi ddaeth!

Becca, by an unknown engraver, c.1842-5.

The Welsh Rioters, published by the *Illustrated London News*, 1843.

Freedom wastes, an eternal prisoner,
    And pain on my pain,
An exile, I begin my journey;
    I am sent from my country,
Land of my father and of my upbringing,
    Into the continent of night,
Over the sea from this safe close,
    Such is my adversity!

This is essentially a traditional ballad of exile, even though it was tied to a contemporary political event. It is soaked through with the maudlin tone of all Welsh protest, resignation in the face of injustice, rather than revolt.

The report of the commissioners sent by the government to investigate the condition of education in Wales in 1847 put a greater strain on loyalty to the English than any other single event in the nineteenth century. It came to be known—in an echo of that first great act of treachery, the Night of the Long Knives—as *Brad y Llyfrau Gleision*, the Treachery of the Blue Books. It stimulated the best integrated written and visualised counter-attack of any in its period, made, like the portrayal of *Brad y Cyllill Hirion* in 1822, by Hugh Hughes.

The observations of the Commissioners on education in Wales were bad enough in themselves, but it was undoubtedly the implication that the nation was also degenerate in religion and morality which stung Welsh intellectual opinion so severely in 1847. In the opinion of the Commissioners, the problem was closely related to Nonconformism and to the Welsh language. As we have seen, the most elevated expression of patriotism for many Nonconformists was the notion that the purity of their reformed religion had set the nation as a whole on a morally higher plane than England. Hugh Hughes, impatient as ever with the early attempts of a

REBECCAITES, OR 'BECCAS.

Y mae ysgrifenwyr galluog, a ffyddlawn dros eu cenedl, yn gwrol ymdrechu i amddiffyn Cymru trwy geisio profi nad yw *ddim gwaeth* na Lloegr....

Fy marn i yw fod clod ac anrhydedd mawr yn deilwng, am fod ein gwlad mewn gwirionedd lawer iawn moesolach nag un genedl sydd yn amddifad o'r grefydd sydd yn ein mysg ni—ond gwelwn mor anhawdd yw cael gan y byd y clod a'r anrhydedd sydd ddyladwy!

stunned intelligentsia at criticism of the reports in the newspapers, remarked:

"Able writers, loyal to their nation, are heroically endeavouring to defend Wales by trying to prove that we are *no worse* than England."

This was utterly inadequate, since:

"In my opinion, praise and great honour are deserved, because our country is in fact much more moral than any nation which is bereft of the religion we have amongst us—but we see how difficult it is to get from the world the praise and honour that is due!"[16]

This remark was made before Ieuan Gwynedd became editor of the newspaper *The Principality* and led the counter attack, and before the historian Jane Williams, Ysgafell, had published her *Remarks on the Reports...* which would put some substance into the indignant reaction by offering statistics that showed that law-breaking, prostitution and the number of children born out of wedlock, were all lower in Wales than in England.

The attack in the Blue Books was upon the two pillars which supported not only the moral base but also the developing superstructure of institutional Welsh distinctness within Britain—education and religion. They came together in the voluntary principle—that is, the right of individual families to educate their children in institutions which reflected their own religious views. This was now threatened by public funding, a matter of fundamental importance to Hugh Hughes and many individualist radicals of the old sort. To their way of thinking, any suggestion of state funding for education was an attack on human rights since they lived in a state which maintained an official religion which they regarded as

Becca, published by the *Illustrated London News*, 1843.

John Jones, Sioni 'Sgubor Fawr, by John Cambrian Rowland, 1839.

Lord John Russell and the Privy Council, by Hugh Hughes, 1848.

decadent. That religion would be imposed on their children, since secular education was a concept with which they were unfamiliar.

The nation was, as ever, misunderstood by the English, in receipt of an undeserved slight. Unfortunately, the evidence on which this injustice was founded had, in a number of cases, been given to the Commissioners by Welsh people—especially priests and landowners. Criticism of such traitors and of fellow-travelling intellectuals who expressed some sympathy with the conclusions of the reports often partook of the bitterness of civil war. Such attacks came close to Hughes himself when his brother-in-law, David Charles, was accused of being "an advocate of the government reports" because he had suggested—as a prominent Methodist—that responsibility for funding education should be transferred to the government. Sometime early in 1848, Hughes therefore determined to publish a series of lithographs under the title *Pictures for the Million of Wales* which would expose, through satire, the malicious intent of the reports. This would be the only occasion on which the medium was used for comment of this kind in this period in Wales. The cartoons were printed at *THE PRINCIPALITY* Office in Cardiff, almost certainly during the six months of Ieuan Gwynedd's editorship. It may well have been Caledfryn, a close friend of both Ieuan Gwynedd and Hugh Hughes, who brought the two together.

Pictures for the Million of Wales, like some of Isaac Thomas's large ballad sheets, were bilingual. The sheets have varying numbers of cartoons, some together with their texts, others with texts separate. The English and Welsh versions vary considerably. In general, the English texts are more sarcastic, taking for granted that the audience is familiar with the characters. Some of the Welsh captions are more explanatory in nature. It was necessary to explain to monoglot Welsh speakers, for instance, the meaning of *Artegall, or The Whipping*, since the work of Jane Williams was not available in Welsh. On the other hand, the dig at the attempts of one of the commissioners, Symons, to learn Welsh, must have had a stronger resonance for Welsh speakers. "Wonders will never cease," remarked a correspondent to *The Principality* in July, 1848.

The cartoons form a narrative history of the Blue Books. In the opening picture, Hughes portrayed Lord John Russell for the second time in his career, though this time fallen from his previous state of grace as the friend of religious freedom. Russell is now the root of all evil, frightening the assembled Lordships in the Privy Council by the assertion that both England and Wales were fast descending into a state of barbarism. Their Lordships are appalled as they are read the letter of a clergyman from Lancashire:

"I asked a boy of six years old (who had been very properly committed to gaol for looking over the stile at the Squire's game)...'WHAT IS YOUR NAME? BILLY. WHAT DID YOUR GODMOTHERS PROMISE FOR YOU IN YOUR BAPTISM? I HASN'T GOT NONE. WHO IS YOUR CLERGYMAN? DON NO. WHO IS THE BISHOP OF YOUR DIOCESE? DON NO. WHAT IS THE NAME OF THE SOVEREIGN OF THESE REALMS? DON NO.' (Sensations of astonishment and horror here seize their Lordships, and their hair stands on end!)...."

The cartoon refers to events nine years previously when the Education Committee of the Privy Council was established, not at that time with the intention exclusively of examining the condition of Wales. The next cartoon shows Sir James Kay-Shuttleworth—Scuttleworth in the cartoon— with a coal scuttle on his head, a pun which must have been lost on the monoglot Welsh speakers. He was in charge of the enquiry and here instructs his three spies, the Commissioners, Lingen, Symons and Johnson, on their duties. Scuttleworth has removed his boots, revealing the cloven hooves of Beelzebub himself. The Commissioners are merely the asinine servants of the Devil, with huge ears poking out from under their wigs. Their brief is clear:

"You are to help their lordships... to make out a case against voluntary religion, by collecting such evidence of its connection with immorality, disloyalty and barbarism, as will disgust the public mind of England, thereby preparing it to sanction the (despotic) scheme in contemplation for driving the Welsh back to the *true Church*. The use of the Welsh LANGUAGE being known to be favourable to the propagation of earnest personal religion, both the LANGUAGE and the NATIONALITY of the Welsh, as well as their religion, are to be destroyed!"

In four cartoons Hughes satirised the way in which the evidence was collected. Of all the evidence given, that emanating from John Griffiths, vicar of Aberdare, aroused the greatest indignation. Since the exact date of the cartoon is unknown, it is not possible to say whether or not Hughes was the first to portray him as a wolf (not exactly in sheep's clothing, though the association is clear), but he became infamous in that character, attacking the flock in his care: "Properly speaking there is no religion whatever in my parish, at least I have not found it yet," he had reported:

"Parson.—This is tolerable wine, Mr. Commissioner—my Church warden is a good fellow, he will pay for this out of the next church rate. With regard to your queries—it is evident to you, from the fact of my drinking parish wine, with a Queen's Commissioner, that there is no religion in this parish, or, at least, that we have no *communicants*. I assure you, I found no religion here, and (he added mentally, while the other was drinking his glass), *I brought none with me*.

"Commissioner. Have the goodness to give me such an account of the morals and manners of the Welsh as I require for the use of their Lordships.

"Parson. All the women of Wales are prostitutes when they have opportunities—and of opportunities they have enough in their prayer meetings. The men and the women are drunken, when they can afford it, and, in order to afford it, they are continually lying, and cheating, and thieving.

"Com. I thank you, Rev. Sir, that's exactly what I want..."

Hughes had referred to the accusation of licentiousness in his fifth cartoon, showing a Peeping Tom looking through a keyhole at night:

"Parson... It is a part of the sacred (secret?) duty of some of the clergy, assisted by their parish clerks, to watch the proceedings of the people in their houses after dark, by peeping through the chinks and key holes; and I have had the pleasure frequently of seeing the women change their under garments—and, *they had but one room!* the men *must* have been there."

In view of the perception that the Blue Books had attacked the morality of Welsh women in particular, it was perhaps appropriate that the first effective counter attack had come from Jane Williams, Ysgafell. Hughes portrayed her as Artegall, the Knight of Justice in the Arthurian legends, whipping the Commissioners, made ludicrous as naughty schoolboys. One of the side effects of the reaction to the reports was increased attention to women's issues in Wales—Ieuan Gwynedd edited the first women's magazine in the Welsh language, *Y Gymraes* (The Welsh-woman), under the patronage of Lady Llanofer, shortly after his brief editorship of *The Principality* came to an end.

The denouement of the story of the Blue Books was also portrayed by Hughes with a strong female emphasis. Lingen, Symons and Johnson are deposited in the sea by Wales in the form of an old woman—the Dame Venodotia of Hughes's earlier popular map of the country. In the tradition of prints dating back to the Commonwealth, Hughes stated that "The accompanying Lithograph is intended to be hung by Welshmen on the walls of their houses, as a memorial of the commencement of the new crusade of Church and State against liberty":

"The very *land*—the *country literally*, which has long *worn the face of humanity*, seems on this occasion, in sympathy with its inhabitants, to have assumed human passion, and threaten to drown the detested slanderers in Cardigan Bay! The streak of solid black down the middle of the print, shows the degree of geographical progress the English *language* has made in a thousand years. Joy is wished to the wiseacres who fondly predict the early extinction of the Welsh language. If the English advances at the same rate in future, the longed for exterpation may be looked for 10,000 years hence! But perhaps a 'paternal' government, under *spiritual* guidance, may find means to hasten the

Dame Venodotia Sousing the Spies, by Hugh Hughes, 1848.

glorious consummation—Could those who speak nothing but Welsh not be prosecuted for speaking at all?..."

Although *Pictures for the Million of Wales* are today certainly the best known nineteenth-century political cartoons, little contemporary comment upon them has come to light. How many were printed and how widely they were distributed remains a mystery. It was the radical writer R.J. Derfel's satirical play, *Brad y Llyfrau Gleision*, that provided the resonant title which encompassed the whole affair. It was published in parts in 1854 in *Yr Amserau* (The Times), until the editor took fright and refused to print the conclusion. Nevertheless, it seems certain from the conception and iconography of the play, which continually echoes Hughes's work, that the cartoons and text were very well known to the playwright.[17]

Following the burst of activity in 1847-8, little use was made by publishers of the abilities of artists and engravers such as Hughes, James Cope, Ellis Owen Ellis and John Roberts for ten years. Apart from an eccentric outburst of letter writing to *Yr Amserau* in 1854-5 and, as a consequence, a sour exchange of insults with William Rees, Gwilym Hiraethog, Hugh Hughes largely faded from the public eye. Cope had disappeared entirely after 1842. Ellis Owen Ellis spent most of his time working in Liverpool and came to public attention only in 1855 with the exhibition of the cartoon for *Oriel y Beirdd*. John Roberts may have been in Dublin—he was certainly engraving there in 1853 when he wrote to John Jones in Llanrwst with an invitation to join him on a visit to the Great Exhibition held in the city in that year.[18] He died, a year later, of tuberculosis, aged only 45. Not until 1858 did a new generation of publishers attempt to bring together satirical writing and images in a popular publication. *Y Punch Cymraeg* was launched in January of that year by Lewis Jones and Evan Jones in partnership in Holyhead. They had not been born when their satirical precursor, the *Figaro in Wales* was closed down in 1836. Behind them stood Richard Evans, Twrch, a clerk in an office in Holyhead, born in 1830. According to Evan Jones, Twrch was responsible for the initial idea

Frontispiece to *Y Punch Cymraeg*, by an unknown engraver, 1858.

and for much of the written material. In its first issue, *Y Punch Cymraeg* offered its readers no political or social manifesto. However, the editorial review of the state of the Welsh nation in January 1858 casually remarked that the week's most important news was the publication of the paper. The editor was probably right. It appeared every fortnight for the next three years, and again, under different proprietors and printed in Liverpool, in 1864. It was aimed at the popular market and priced at 1d. Although *Y Punch Cymraeg* interested itself in stories from the whole of Wales, it had a strong bias towards Gwynedd and Liverpool, suggesting that the writers of most of its material were working in those two areas, in touch with inside information and local gossip. Nevertheless, as with the *Figaro* (and doubtless for the same reasons), precisely who those writers were—apart from Twrch—remains obscure.

The magazine's first signed cartoon was also the work of Twrch, a tidily engraved comment on the fashion for crinolines with huge bustles. It may well have been drawn by a professional engraver to his idea, after the manner of Thomas Pennant's cartoons. Twrch perhaps devised other, unsigned, cartoons for *Y Punch Cymraeg* but the majority of the large number which appeared from March 1858 on were the work of Ellis Owen Ellis, variously signed "Bryn Coch" or "Ellis Bryn Coch". Like Twrch, he followed the long tradition of popular comment on the absurdities of fashion with cartoons on the subject of crinolines, notably his *Peiriannau Ysgubo Heolydd* (Street Cleaning Machines), published in August, 1858. Two disgruntled street cleaners of the old sort, with besoms, watch the new crinoline technology in action, sweeping all before it including the

"MAE Y FAN YMA CYSTAL A'R SPRING SOFFA A DORAIS DDOE WRTH YMSTWYRIAN."

TWRCH.

dirty face of a chimney sweep who happens to be on the pavement at the time. The lengthy text, in this case including three separate anecdotes, is characteristic of the way *Y Punch Cymraeg* used words with pictures. Only a very few cartoons stand without extended written comment. However, the relationship between writer and cartoonist is not clear. Ellis's work is usually so closely integrated with the text that it is difficult to see either one as simply an illustration of the other. They carry the hallmarks of having been worked out co-operatively, a process involving considerable logistical difficulties in the period, since the printers and the main satirist were in Holyhead and the artist in Liverpool. It seems likely, therefore, that in some cases, at least, both text and cartoon were the work of Ellis Owen Ellis. A rare surviving letter from the artist concerning *Oriel y Beirdd* has echoes of the florid, self-mocking style of *Punch* texts. The letter is ostensibly a straightforward note of thanks to Miss Davies, Penmaen Dyfi, for the loan of Hugh Hughes' portrait of her uncle, Gwallter Mechain, on which his portrait in *Oriel y Beirdd* was based, but it comes dangerously close to a send-up of the respectable lady and her famous ancestor:

"Regarding the Portrait of the immortal Gwallter Mechain I beg to state that I have commenced operation thereon; not only that I intend taking pains to execute the portrait in a style of masterly superiority but that I am resolved that it shall be presented to the public in the full conviction that it will contain a faithful representation of the departed great in his Canonicals..."[19]

Ellis Owen Ellis's images are distinct in style. They lack the elegant composition of James Cope's work, reflecting more closely the literal

The Spring Sofa, by Richard Evans, Twrch, 1858.

Richard Evans, Twrch, by Ellis Owen Ellis, 1860.

147

Hen wrageddos, neu waelach na hyny—canys bydd hen wrageddos yn siarad, ond am seneddwyr Cymru, nis gallant godi cyd-rhyngddynt gymaint o ysbryd a chyw gwydd neu hen iâr yn clowcian!

1. Esgobion Cymreig i'r Eglwys Gymreig...
2. Barnwyr Cymreig...
3. Rhaid i ni gael *pob swydd gyhoeddus yn Nghymru*—o'r Esgob i'r *Postman*... i gael ei llenwi gan Gymry.

Peirianau Ysgubo Heolydd, by Ellis Owen Ellis, 1858.

construction of visual elements into a story which was characteristic of Isaac Thomas's work in Cardigan. His first cartoon for *Y Punch Cymraeg* (and one of his finest), was directed against the old enemy, the English church. He attacked it both as the agent of Anglicisation in Wales and of covert popery. They would have seemed to Ellis to come to much the same thing. Three of the four bishops—Short, Bothwell, and Ollivant—are whipped over Offa's Dyke and into a fiery dragon's mouth by Richard Williams Morgan, curate of Tregynon, who holds a leek. The image is accompanied by a spoof quotation from the Koran, headed "Cyflawniad y Proffwydoliaethau" (Fulfilment of the Prophecies):

"And at the end of the year of 1857, one of the name MORGANS came forth, and gathered up pieces of the Chain of Succession,—which had broken as a result of too many Puseyites trying to climb up it to the land of glory, and he bound the three men on the back of the *Stallion of Death,* and sent them straight into the whirlpool! And then there was peace on earth for a thousand years."

The Welsh curate who drove his Puseyite employers back to England, from where they had come, was a patriotic poet and polemicist. Less than a year before, he had published *The British Kymry or Britons of Cambria,* translated into Welsh by his friend John Williams, Ab Ithel, and he was about to publish *Amddiffiniad yr Iaith Gymraeg* (A Defence of the Welsh Language), in which he attacked the use of the English language by the Established Church in Wales. The pamphlet was made up of two letters, recently published in the *Caernarvon and Denbigh Herald* (the antidote to the "Palace Gazette"), with an introduction. They had originally gone under the title "Yr Iaith Gymraeg i Gymru" (The Welsh Language for Wales), and in them, Morgan outspokenly attacked both his ecclesiastical employers and toothless Welsh Members of Parliament for failing to assert the nation's interests in London. They were:

"...old women, or worse than that—because at least old women say something, but Welsh parliamentarians, they couldn't raise between them as much spirit as a gosling or a clucking old hen."[20]

Cyflawniad y Proffwyd-oliaethau, by Ellis Owen Ellis, 1858.

He demanded of the "English government" the old Cymreigyddion agenda, publicised in *Y Cymro* a quarter of a century before:

"1. Welsh Bishops for the Welsh Church...
2. Welsh judges...
3. We must have *every public office in Wales*—from the Bishop to the *Postman... filled by Welsh people.*"

Consistent with Morgan's letters to the *Herald,* the text of Ellis's cartoon set the radical and patriotic agenda of *Y Punch Cymraeg,* maintained through-out its existence. It is unambiguously anti-English, a distinct change of tone when compared to the cautious efforts of the older generation, before the trauma of the Blue Books:

"Stick at it, Death! You're serving a nation today. Over Offa's Dyke at a gallop fly the arrogant plunderers who have been shameless enough to take tens of thousands of pounds of the people's money year after year, when they know, yes, they *know* that the Almighty has never fitted them to labour in the Welsh Vineyard. They are foreign to the feelings, the language and the national customs of the Welsh; and mortal enemies to

Self-portrait, by Ellis Owen Ellis, 1860.

everything with a Welsh quality to it. In fact, the plague of English Bishops in Wales is just one instance of the everlasting enmity of the English to the language and nationality of the Welsh. And how can officers bred like this in treachery, and who keep their thrones through violence, expect the blessing of Heaven on their work? Poor devils, they think that the mere tinkling of the Chain of Succession in the ears of the simple Welsh will bring them rushing back to their old Mother like a swarm of bees back to the hive. This is their mistake: they treat the Welsh more like irrational animals than men that from the womb, through the Sunday School, know the Holy Scriptural way to salvation. But where is the fourth Bishop? To the great comfort of the inhabitants of the South, they have one there who can recite the Welsh Shibboleth, and so he was spared. But as for the other three, they have been carefully saddled as pillions of Death, who knows exactly where to take them.

> 'God will ensure they don't return
> To bewitch and try his children.'

And if they or their ghosts do return, Mr. Morgan has made a covenant with death to send them back for a thousand years, the Sort next to death, Both-in-hell, and the Elephant."

The Bishops proved to have considerably more staying power than *Y Punch Cymraeg* or Morgan would have liked. These were determined evangelicals—Ollivant the first bishop to reside at Llandaf for centuries and a builder (and rebuilder) of churches on a large scale, and Short of St Asaph, an educationalist who saw to it that every parish in his care acquired a school, and—contrary to the suggestion in *Y Punch Cymraeg*—who provided bilingual textbooks, though not, one supposes, out of a desire to see the language flourish.

As we have seen, Evan Lloyd would have had difficulty in recognising nineteenth-century Welsh radicalism which was anything but libertarian. The puritan strain was often to the fore in the cartoons and texts in *Y Punch Cymreig*. Ellis Owen Ellis had an impeccable Methodist pedigree.[21] What was, in fact, a spoof biblical passage against the bishops, was carefully transferred to the Koran to avoid accusations of taking the word of God in vain, for instance, a fine example of the humbug that the magazine liked to attack in others. *Y Punch Cymreig* took a dim view of sports, and —as in James Cope's attack on the Bishop of Bangor in 1841—associated them with the English church in a cartoon entitled *Sports i'r Cenedloedd—Y ffordd BERSONOL i ddiwygio'r byd* (Games for the Gentiles—the

Y FFORDD **BERSONOL** I DDIWYGIO'R BYD.

Y CYNLLUN DUWIOL AT LEIHAU DYLED CAPEL GARSTON.

PERSONAL way to reform the world). However, Mr Punch was aware that such regressive tendencies were not the sole prerogative of the English church. When Welsh Methodists in Liverpool took steps to reduce the debts incurred in the building of Garston chapel by organising a lottery, they found themselves on the receiving end of the magazine's sarcasm and a cartoon. Nevertheless, the English were again seriously implicated, and Dic Siôn Dafyddism was the ultimate target. The Welsh text has a smattering of buzz words in English, in mock of the speech of the upwardly mobile:

"THE LIVERPOOL RELIGIOUS LOTTERY—REPORT OF THE COMMITTEE.

Sports i'r Cenedloedd!, by Ellis Owen Ellis, 1858.

Y Cynllun Duwiol at Leihau Dyled Capel Garston, by Ellis Owen Ellis, 1858.

WOULD-BE BLAENOR [wrtho ei hun]: "Areithiodd fy nghyf-aill yn frwd o blaid yr achos dirwestol, a bu hyny yn *stepping-stone* iddo i'r cysegr nesaf i mewn; mi wnaf finau yr un peth. Daeth allan yn ngrym ei hyawdledd i gondemnio a damnio y ta-farnwyr a'r bragwyr n holl ger y diafol, a bu hyny yn ris iddo i'r flaenoriaeth; mi wnaf finau yr un peth. Areithiodd yn galed yn y Cyfarfodydd Llenyddol, a bu hyny yn ddyrchafiad iddo yn ngo-lwg pobl yn scwintio: mi wnaf finau yr un peth. Daeth allan yn holl fawredd ei athrylith i humbugio mewn ethol-iadau, a gwelodd Sion Gorph ei fedr-usrwydd, a dyrchafodd ef i'r swydd anrhydeddus o B, C. (Blaenor y Corph); mi waaf finau yr un peth. Mewn gair, dylynaf ol ei droed mewn pob dim, a phwy a wyr felly na welir finau yn enol yr hyfrydwch a'r fraint o gyrhaedd prif nod fy mywyd, sef esgyn o blith yr *hum-bugs* cyffredin yma i eistedd ar orseddfa y flaenoriaeth, ac ysgwyd teyrnwialen yr eglwys nes y bo corachod "y llawr" yn swatio yn fy ngwydd, a gosod fy ofn a'm harswyd ar bawb a phobpeth na fyddont o'r unfarn a mi, ac esgymuno i ddiafol bob aelod a feiddio godi llef yn erbyn fy nghyfrifon."

A WOULD-BE Blaenor yn dylyn ol traed Hwsmon gyda Sion Gorph.

LOTRI CREFYDDOL LERPWL—ADRODDIAD Y PWYLLGOR.
Teimla eich Pwyllgor yn llawen yn cyflwyno yr adroddiad hwn wrth feddwl am y llwyddiant a ddilynodd eu hanturiaeth. Pan ddaeth yr *idea* gyntaf trwy ddychymyg Miss Dorcas, Rose Place, yr oedd pawb yn ei gymeradwyo, a phawb yn ofni nad allesid ei weithio allan. Yr oedd yn dwyn cymaint o sawyr Seisnig arno fel yr oedd agos bawb yn ei hoffi, gan fod ynom awydd i fod yn debyg iddynt yn mhob peth. Yr oedd y cynllun hefyd yn fagwraeth fendithiol i

elfen wareiddiol arall sydd yn cynyddu yn ein plith, sef cyfleusdra at *useful recreation* ac *innocent amusement*. Bu adeg yn amseroedd tywyll Methodistiaeth pan edrychid ar hyny yn bechod, ac y gwirdroid Rheol vi yn ein 'Cyffes Ffydd' anffaeledig i brofi hyny. Ond trwy drugaredd mae y cyfnod barbaraidd hwnw wedi myned heibio, ac nid oes mwyach yn aros ond ambell i hen flaenor pengam wedi ei adael fel cof-golofn o dywyllwch sylfaenwyr Methodistiaeth....

A Would-be Blaenor..., by Ellis Owen Ellis, 1860.

"Your Committee is delighted to present this report in view of the success that attended our venture. When the first *idea* sprung into the imagination of Miss Dorcas, Rose Place,[22] everyone approved of it, though everyone feared that it could not be made to work. It had such an English odour hanging about it, that nearly everybody liked it, since we so much desire to be similar to them in all things. The plan was also a useful nursery for another civilising element which is growing amongst us, that is the convenience of *useful recreation* and *innocent amusement*. There was a time in the dark period of Methodism when this was looked upon as a sin, and Rule vi in our infallible Confession of Faith was overturned to prove the point. But, mercifully, that barbaric period has passed, and nowadays there is only the occasional stubborn old deacon left behind as a monument to the ignorance of the founders of Methodism..."

Dic Siôn Dafydd-ism and the gratuitous use of the English language as a symbol of social elevation, were often lampooned in *Y Punch Cymraeg*, especially in the context of the Nonconformist churches in their mid-century mood of self-satisfaction. The Nonconformist social ladder had become the one to climb, and especially the Methodist ladder. Mr Punch attacked the resultant pretensions with energy, creating the character of Sion Gorph to embody the Methodist hierarchy. An Ellis cartoon of 1860, *A WOULD-BE Blaenor yn dylyn ol traed Hwsmon gyda Sion Gorph* (A

WOULD-BE Deacon following in the footsteps of Hwsmon with Sion Gorph) attacked the social aspirations of the Methodist laity:

Y Ddau Allu, by Ellis Owen Ellis, 1859.

"WOULD-BE DEACON (to himself): My friend spoke eloquently for the temperance cause, and that was a *stepping-stone* for him towards the next inner-sanctum; I'm going to do the same thing. He came out with the full force of his rhetoric to condemn and damn by the devil all the publicans and the brewers, and that was a step up for him on the way to a deaconship; I'm going to do the same thing. He spoke forcefully in the Literary Meeting, and that elevated him in the estimation of the squinting fraternity; I'm going to do the same thing. He uttered humbug with great philosophical force in the elections, and Sion Gorph perceived his talent, and elevated him to the honoured position of B.C. (Blaenor y Corff, i.e. deacon of the Church); I'm going to do the same thing. In a word, I'm going to follow everywhere in his footsteps, and who knows, I too may have the pleasure and the honour of securing the main objective of my life, to ascend from the ranks of these common *humbugs* to sit on the throne of the deaconship, and rattle the sceptre of the church until the midgets below quake at my presence, and frighten and terrorise everyone and everything that isn't of the same mind as me, and excommunicate to the devil every member who dares to question my accounts."

Any undignified internal wranglings within the "spiritual empire of Method-istia" that, in the opinion of Mr Punch, set itself up as the moral arbiter of the nation, were a source of great delight. In its annual meeting in the summer of 1858, the Methodist Missionary Society had been presented with a number of critical motions, in particular from Môn and Arfon, concerning the alleged failure of the Reverend John Mills, missionary to the Jewish community in London, to achieve conversions. The spiritual condition of the Jews was a matter of intense interest to evangelicals in the period, with stories of individual conversions almost anywhere in the world reported in minute detail in the religious press. John Mills came under suspicion as a fellow-traveller not simply because of his practical failure but because of his sympathetic reports of the Jewish way of life published in *Y Drysorfa* (The Treasury), the denominational magazine. To evangelicals they seemed to be an apologia for Jewish attitudes rather than a Christian

153

Dy(m)chweliad yr Iddewon, by Ellis Owen Ellis, 1859.

condemnation. John Mills had become the acknowledged gentile expert on British Jewry, publishing *Iddewon Prydain* (The British Jews) in 1852, translated into English the following year, and *Palestina* in 1858. Matters were further polarised by the existence of an old dispute between fundamentalist and liberal Christians about how best to achieve conversion—"dadl y ddau allu"—the argument of the two powers. In April, 1859, in a long piece accompanied by an Ellis cartoon, *Y Punch Cymraeg* satirised "the *niceties and fine subtleties* of the two shools of thought, each splendid one of them." John Mills clearly belonged to the "moral" school of gentle persuasion, and Mr Punch took his part in the dispute against the proponents of "the law of the big stick", as the paper put it. In the annual meeting in 1858, Mills was severely criticised, the occasion of the *Punch* cartoon. Sion Gorph, in the chair, looses his temper with the wimpish liberal intellectuals defending John Mills:

"The Chairman arose, his eyes flashing with anger, and having given the boot to the Missionary, grabbed the Jew's beard and commenced to drag him unceremoniously to the Cross. It was difficult to know who was shouting the most. 'A human halter for me,' said the Chairman, 'and no more of your moral means, if you please.' In the middle of this scene, the conservatives broke into the following verse, which was sung with heavenly *hwyl*:

When others toil with philosophic force,
Our nimble sense will take a shorter course—
Fling at your head conviction by the lump,
And gain remote conclusions at a jump."

The unfortunate John Mills resigned in a letter published in *Y Drysorfa*, whose dense and sober pages were a fine source of humbug for Mr Punch's satire. The paper followed up its first attack with a second cartoon by Ellis Owen Ellis in which the pig of Môn and the goat of Arfon draw the coffin of John Mills and the London Jewish mission under the title *DY(M)CHWELIAD YR IDDEWON*, a pun on the word for conversion which is similar to the word for destruction. A cheery Sion Gorph is the undertaker as Justice looks on askance from the sidelines.

Methodistia was not amused, and determined on a counter attack, delivered rather through the back door from the platform of the annual meeting of the Anglesey Sunday Schools. The Kremlin-like *modus operandi* of the Methodists in Association and their paranoid reaction to criticism in the press was the subject of an Ellis cartoon entitled *"YMOSODIAD BEIDDGAR 'Y CORFF' AR AMDDIFFYNFA RHYDDID Y WASG"*—the arrogant attack of "Methodistia" on the castle of press freedom. While the newspapers *Baner Cymru, Yr Udgorn,* and the *Herald* circle above, Mr Punch, with historically conscious iconography, defends the freedom of the press. He is mounted on Poor Taff's goat and fires quill pens as arrows after the style of Hugh Hughes. His establishment target is substantially embodied in the person of Thomas Gee, press baron of Methodistia, and indeed of Wales as a whole. *Y Drysorfa* was his instrument of oppression:

"...it was there that the judgement was published as to whether any book should be read, or not—deciding the fate of some book became one of the most important "decisions" of the assembly,—its condemnation was a death sentence and its recommendation assured success. The country began to be swamped with controversial screeds written by starving and unstable (and unestablished) ministers, but all carrying the privileged imprint and so selling like hot cakes. One of the first to be hung was the Bardd Cwsg[23] and the latest that they *sought* to hang was poor Mr Punch..."

Although the Methodists were the chief object of scrutiny in *Y Punch Cymraeg*, other Nonconformist denominations were not exempt. The opening of the new St Pauls Schools in Bangor attracted considerable comment because of the generally self-righteous tone of the proceedings and, in particular, the excessive flattery by the Wesleyans of their benefactor, Evan Evans, Erw Fair. The populace had their doubts about the much-vaunted amenability and sobriety of this gentleman, and the magazine published two articles with cartoons under the title *"Te Parti Capel y Botel"* (The Bottle Chapel Tea Party). *The North Wales Chronicle* had reported the Wesleyan grovellings with approval, but *Y Punch Cymraeg* produced a rather different version. Ellis Owen Ellis's second cartoon showed a bloated Evans wearing an inane grin suggesting that his teacup had contained something rather stronger than tea. "The Palace Gazette" had laid great emphasis on the prominent place given to "that delightful beverage"[24] at the opening ceremony. Among those depicted by Ellis greasing various parts of Evans' anatomy were the Reverend Samuel Davies, Llanfyllin, and David Evans, the builder. Mr Evans had

Ymosodiad Beiddgar "Y Corff" ar Amddiffynfa Rhyddid y Wasg, by Ellis Owen Ellis, 1858.

155

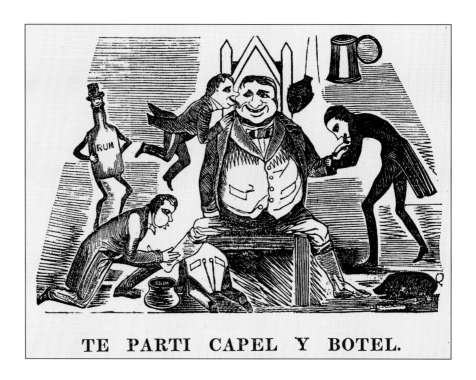

TE PARTI CAPEL Y BOTEL.

Te Parti Capel y Botel, by Ellis Owen Ellis, 1859.

been moved to respond in his speech to the suggestions at large in Bangor that the benefactor was not such a shining light as he liked to be portrayed. "He spoke from conscientious motives as a rumour had gone forth that Mr Evans was of a different character." Chief among the acolytes was the Reverend William Davies, who was minister at Beaumaris and therefore satirised by Mr Punch as Y Gwir Barchedig Mr Cocklebeau. He was among the most prominent Wesleyans of the period:

"Oh how I shake in my boots as I mention the man who adressed us next! Oh fellow citizens! doff your caps—bow politely, and grovel in the dust before him, because his name it is wonderful—*The Right Reverend Mr Cocklebeau!*—the man for whom the creation shook, the waves of the deep were stilled—the stars were darkened, the heavens sent forth lightning, and the heights of the heavens their thunder—the angels rejoiced and the devils of the Great Irrevocable were terrified—when the bell of the 'Church in the Air'[25] announced his birth—this is the being that great *Nature* has searched a thousand years to find materials suitable for his construction: and having found them and finished the design, she was in such haste to see a little perfection on the playground of time, that unfortunately she pulled him from the *mould* before he was complete!"

A regular feature of *Y Punch Cymraeg* from its inception was the satire of contemporary eisteddfod poets in the cartoon and column "*Yr Arddangosfa Farddonol*" *(The Poetic Exhibition)*. The exhibition in question was a fairground freak-show run by one Barnum, a pun on the name of the famous circus proprietor, the first syllable of which—*barn*—means "opinion" or "judgement", and has distinctly cataclysmic overtones. Barnum (= Judge 'em) and his audience are common to all the cartoons whose subjects included such luminaries as John Jones, Talhaiarn—a favourite target in *Y Punch Cymraeg* as he combined High

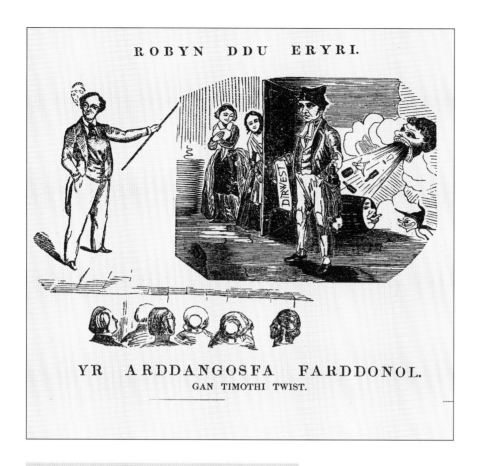

ROBYN DDU ERYRI.

YR ARDDANGOSFA FARDDONOL.
GAN TIMOTHI TWIST.

pob dyn od yng Nghymru wedi ei hel ei hun yno,
ac y mae'n debyg eu bod yn teimlo'n gwbl
gartrefol yn y cwmni.

Church views with an inclination to drink. Twrch had strong temperance convictions, and we may safely presume that he was Timothi Twist, author of the satires. Robert Parry, Robin Ddu Eryri, another victim of the column, led a rather wandering existence, both physically and intellectually, with little visible means of financial support. Ellis Owen Ellis, therefore, portrayed him ragged, and with clerical bands, presumably to indicate his fondness for preaching. However, the main allusion was to the fact that Robin Ddu had acquired a high reputation as a speaker on temperance platforms, despite being—like Talhaiarn—given to the bottle.

In the autumn of the first year of the publication of *Y Punch Cymraeg*, the extraordinary Llangollen Eisteddfod met. Isaac Foulkes, Llyfrbryf, remarked that "every odd-bod in Wales took himself off there, and no doubt felt quite at home in the company."[26] Characteristic of a strong contingent of Glamorgan oddities was William Price of Pontypridd who was in the habit of dressing up in druidical robes to perform mysterious ceremonies by the ancient stone on the common. In an earlier and more worldly incarnation he had been prominent among the Chartists at Newport in 1839. The Eisteddfod was the conception of John Williams, Ab Ithel, Evan Davies, Myfyr Morganwg, and Richard Williams Morgan, Môr Meirion—hero of Ellis's first cartoon for the magazine, attacking the English bishops. This triumvirate, steeped in druidical mumbo-jumbo, was determined to cement together Iolo Morganwg's Gorsedd and the Eisteddfod movement, first associated at Carmarthen in 1819. Just about everything at Llangollen was controversial, and especially the choice of adjudicators and their decisions. Ab Ithel himself won a £30 prize, and his son and daughter were also well-rewarded for their creativity. Druidical robes were worn for the ceremonies, led on the stage by the curate of Tregynon. One of the most unusual manifestations in a generally unusual event was the appearance of the Archdruid, Myfyr Morganwg, with a "mundane egg", presumably fossilized, hanging on a string about his

Robyn Ddu Eryri, by Ellis Owen Ellis, 1859.

157

neck. It was alleged that this item had been dug up in a druidical grave near Llandaf some four hundred years since, and contained the spirits of the children of Ceridwen. In Ellis Owen Ellis's lampoon of the proceedings, Ab Ithel—in the guise of a large bird of indeterminate species—sits upon the egg, from which have hatched assorted Celtic deities. The *nod cyfrin* (secret sign), made of rather worm-eaten wood being surveyed by a snail, hangs above his head. To the right a March hare is playing—both Celtic god and Saxon symbol of madness.

The imagery of Ellis Owen Ellis stands at the tip of the long shadow cast by the seventeenth-century woodcut tradition through which the culture of Wales was visualised for the first time. Images such as *Y Ddau Haman Cymreig* (The Two Welsh Hamans) are the linear descendants of a medieval iconography common to all Europe, reintroduced to Wales by James Cope. They were made at the very end of the career of Ellis Owen Ellis, and although *Y Punch Cymraeg* found other cartoonists for its brief reappearance in 1864, with his death the tradition came to an end. Political and social satire in the form of the cartoon would flourish again in Wales, notably in the drawings of J.M. Staniforth in the *Western Mail* at the turn of the century. However, the context of the newspaper was a different one, where satirical comment was self-contained in the cartoon, and texts carried reportage and analysis. The tradition of words with pictures had a more direct descendant by the end of the nineteenth century in early cinemas which toured the fairs as popular entertainment, just as the ballad singers had done before them. The silent films of William Haggar, with captions between the scenes, reflected the subject matter and imagery of the popular press. In Haggar's *The Life of Charles Peace*, made in 1905, is a hanging scene in the same vein as that published by John Jones in *Bywyd Turpin Leidr*, illustrated by Ellis Owen Ellis, seventy years before.[27]

The Christmas supplement to *Y Punch Cymraeg* in 1858 published an unusual print by Ellis Owen Ellis—not a comment on contemporary events but an allegory of change in the moralising tradition of the ballad sheet. From under the cloak of Eternity the old year extends her hand in farewell to Father Time—"Old Time, grey haired and crooked"—while the virgin future pushes forward at his feet to ask his favour:

Messrs. Tom, Satan, & Jack, Flour, Brimstone, and
Cotton Ball Merchants.
Neu Y DDAU HAMAN CYMREIG.

Bydd gan Mr. Punch ddarlun o Pantomine Capel y Dwndwr, Bangor,
yn ei rifyn nesaf, yn nghyda bras-linelliad o'r chwareu a'r chwareu-
wyr doniol.

" Dan dywyll fantell tragwyddoldeb mawr
Y flwydd drancedig a estyna 'i llaw,
I ganu'n iach a'i thad, Hen Amser penllwyd, crwm ;
Tra wrth ei gwt yr ie'ngaf un o'i blant,
Dan wenu fel morwynig, wthia'n mlaen
I ddysgwyl am ei ffafrau."

Under the dark mantle of eternity
The spent year extends her hand,
To wish old Father Time, grey-haired and crooked, well;
While at his feet the youngest of his children,
With virgin smile, comes forward,
Hoping for his favour.

Y Ddau Haman Cymreig,
by Ellis Owen Ellis, 1860.

Eternity, by Ellis Owen
Ellis, 1858.

Notes

I

1. For John Jones, see G. Morgan, *Y Dyn a Wnaeth Argraff*, Llanrwst, 1982.

2. London—674,000 in 1700 (G.M. Trevelyan, *English Social History*, London, 1973, p.343), Wales—360,000 in 1620 rising to 500,000 in 1770 (John Davies, *Hanes Cymru*, London, 1990, p.302).

3. For Thomas Jones, see Geraint H. Jenkins, "Almanaciau Thomas Jones, 1680-1717", *Ysgrifau Beirniadol*, XIV, 1988. Jenkins quotes (p.196) the verses given from the *Almanac am y flwydddyn 1693*. For the growth of literacy, see Aneurin Lewis, "Llyfrau Cymraeg a'u Darllenwyr, 1696-1740", *Efrydiau Athronyddol*, 1971.

4. *Cymru* OME, XXII, 1902, p.10. Ywain Meirion was Owen Griffith, 1803-1868. The spelling of his name varies from source to source. This text follows: Tegwyn Jones, *Baledi Ywain Meirion*, Bala, 1980.

   To accompany his picture of Aberystwyth Fair, Samuel Ireland wrote: "At the market or fair, the usual artifices to amuse and delude were exhibited with the usual success; other centuries revolve, and other generations arise but rustic manners remain unchanged, the same pursuits occupy the mind, and the same toys interest and beguile. There were 'Ribbands of all the colors ith' rainbow. Dancing and music, ballads all pitiful and true...'." S. Ireland, *Picturesque Views on the River Wye*, 1797.

5. *Cymru* OME, XXVII, 1904, p.166-7.

6. Robert Griffith, *Deueg o Feirdd y Berwyn*, 1910. *Datgeiniad* means the one who recites or performs; *penpasdwn* refers to the ball or crook on the top of his staff.

7. Thomas Pennant, *Tours in Wales*, ed. John Rhys, Caernarfon, 1883, II, p.101.

8. The complex system of alliteration within a line which characterises the strict metres of Welsh language poetry.

9. Tegwyn Jones, op. cit., p.ix.

10. Thomas Davies, *Dinas Mawddwy a'i Hamgylchoedd*, 1893, p.68-70.

11. UCW Bangor, Ms.5709 (5), letter dated 29 January 1845. For Roos, see Peter Lord, *Artisan Painters*, Aberystwyth, 1993.

12. NLW Ms.12021C, and following quotation.

13. Hugh Hughes and David Charles, *Yr Addysgydd*, Carmarthen, 1823, "Atodiad." For Hugh Hughes, see Peter Lord, *Hugh Hughes, Arlunydd Gwlad*, Llandysul, 1995.

14. William Hone, *Ancient Mysteries Described*, London, 1832, p.100, quoted in Leslie Shepard, *John Pitts, Ballad Printer of Seven Dials*, London, 1969.

15. Margaret Lambert and Enid Marx, *English Popular and Traditional Art*, London, 1946, p.7. Noel Carrington, *Popular Art in Britain*, London, 1945, makes similar observations.

    John Selden was an early collector of broadside ballads: "Though some make slight of libels, yet you may see by them how the wind sits. As take a straw and throw it up into the air, you shall see by that which way the wind is, which you shall not do by casting up a stone. More solid things do not show the complexion of the times so well as ballads and libels." See Leslie Shepard, *The Broadside Ballad*, London, 1962, p.102.

16. Tegwyn Jones, op. cit., p.xxxiv.

17. *Cymru* OME, XXII, op. cit.

18. The ballad is no.166 in NLW, Sir John Williams collection. John Cadwalad was presumably the John Kadwaladr or Siôn Cadwaladr who also wrote interludes. He was from Llanycil, Meirionydd, but spent seven years in exile in America for the theft of half a crown.

19. The survival of a ballad in printed form cannot be taken as evidence of its popularity. Some patrons or writers with a personal axe to grind could pay for work to be printed.

20. *CAN NEWYDD Yn nghylch y terfysg a gymerodd le yn nhref Cas'newydd...*, published by John Jones, Llanrwst.

21. Linda Colley, *Britons. Forging the Nation 1707 - 1837*, London, 1992, makes much of the common bond of Protestant Christianity in encouraging loyalty to the idea of Britain. I believe this to be an Anglo-centric perception which ignores the proprietorial attitude of Welsh intellectuals to the idea which was the most important source of their loyalty. It also ignores the fact that the continuing sense of national distinctness in Wales was reinforced by sectarian divisions within Protestantism: see below.

22. *Cerdd ar Undeb a gymmerodd le rhwng y Cymry a'r Saeson* (un o destunau blynyddol Cymdeithas Gymreigyddawl Nant Padarn, 1826).

23. On 27 September 1820, Hugh Hughes spent "three or four hours" in the company of John Hughes and Ifor Ceri. A review of *Horae Britannicae* in the *Cambro-Briton*, 1821, p.326, quotes Hughes's description of the event at length. The medal awarded as a prize by the Gwent Cymreigyddion was engraved with a picture of Stonehenge.

24. *European Magazine*, XVIII (1790), p.168.

25. See Peter Lord, "The Bard—Celticism and Visual Culture", *Gwenllian—Essays on Visual Culture*, Llandysul, 1994. In his study of the theme in *The Image of Antiquity*, Yale, 1994, Sam Smiles demonstrates the same Anglo-centric understanding as Linda Colley, op. cit.. He does not indicate that Welsh perceptions of the Bard and the Druid differed in important ways from the perceptions of the English; nor does he discuss any of the numerous nineteenth and early twentieth-century Welsh versions of the image.

26. For example, the story of the painting of David Williams, Troedrhiwdalar, in *Y Tyst a'r Dydd*, 18 December 1874, p.2-3.

27. Unidentified newspaper cutting in Samuel Morris Jones's scrapbook, Gwynedd Archives, Caernarfon.

28. *Tlysau'r Hen Oesoedd*, 1735, the introduction.

29. *Cronicl y Cymdeithasau Crefyddol*, XVI, 1858, p.106.

S.R. made this comment in a cautionary foreword to a review by an anonymous writer of the Manchester art exhibition, opened the previous year.

30. Hugh Hughes and David Charles, op. cit., November, 1823. The apologia was made in the context of an engraving by Hughes of St Peter healing the lame man—the first time that a subject from the New Testament had been illustrated in the *Addysgydd*.

31. *Yr Athraw i Blentyn*, printed by John Jones, Llanrwst, 1827. The comment is made in the foreword, signed by J. Edwards, R. Williams, J. Prichard and Ellis Evans.

II

1. Taffy was a Welshman, Taffy was a thief,
   Taffy came to my house and stole a leg of beef...

   The rhyme is first recorded in *Nancy Cook's Pretty Song Book*, c.1780. *The Companion to Welsh Literature*, ed. Meic Stephens, Cardiff, 1986, associates the rhyme with Flemish immigration into Pembrokeshire. See under "Taffy".

2. Quoted in W.J. Hughes, *Wales and the Welsh in English Literature*, Wrexham, 1924. The spellings differ from those given in E. Vincent Evans, "Andrew Boorde and the Welsh People", *Y Cymmrodor*, XXIV, 1919.

3. Reprinted in E. Vincent Evans, ibid.

4. Cymro, "Cursory Remarks on Welsh Tours or Travels", *Cambrian Register*, 1796.

5. *Henry V*, Act I, Scene 2.

6. Thomas Matthews, *The Biography of John Gibson*, 1911, p.190.

7. Thomas Pennant, op. cit., II, p.301.

8. Thomas Matthews, op. cit., p.189.

9. Quoted in Arthur E. Hughes, "The Welsh National Emblem: Leek or Daffodil", *Y Cymmrodor*, XXVI, 1916.

10. *Henry V*, Act IV, Scene 7.

11. Ibid. Act V, Scene 1.

12. P.29.

13. *Y Brython*, second edition, p.359.

14. Arthur E. Hughes, op. cit., p.172.

15. J.R. Phillips, *Memoirs of the Civil War*, p.128.

16. A. Grace Roberts, "Archbishop Williams", *Welsh Outlook*, 1926, p.38.

17. Ibid.

18. William Lilly, *Mr Lilly's History of his Life and Times*, London, 1721, p.21-3.

19. That is, he adjudicated in disputes on the basis that his supernatural powers would enable him to say where the truth lay. He might also predict where lost objects were to be found.

20. James Howell, *The Parly of Beasts; or Morphandra, Queen of the Inchanted Iland*, 1660, p.122, and the epigram following. James Howell, 1593-1666, was born in Abernant, Caernarfonshire.

21. P.3, in NLW DA 1241 T67. Another edition has consecutive pagination through the pamphlets.

22. William Richards, *Wallography, or the Briton Described*, 1682, p.81-2.

23. Anon., "A Trip to North-Wales...", *A Collection of Welsh Travels*, published by J. Torbuck, 1738, p.15.

24. Thomson to David Mallet, published in *Miscellany of the Philobiblian Society*, IV, (1857-8), 20.

III

1. John Ireland, *Hogarth Illustrated*, 1791, I, p.43.

2. For the election, see P.D.G. Thomas, "Wynnstay versus Chirk Castle", *NLW Journal*, 11, 1959, p.117.

3. That is, a Pasha or provincial governor, suggesting the reward he expected for his sedition.

4. Trial, BM 6485, aaa.21-2.

5. So called after young men returning from the Grand Tour with their heads full of Italian fashions.

6. *Freeholder's Magazine*, II, March 1770, p.41.

7. Patch had painted a caricature group of Sir Watkin and his associates two years previously.

8. The copy in NLW is inscribed in an old hand "Sir Watkin Williams Wynn 1771". For the reasons given, however, both the identification and the date are dubious. The text suggests that the subject may have had something to do with publishing.

9. *Middlesex Journal*, 29 April 1769.

10. Cardiff City Library, Ms.3.18, ff.33-5.

11. The suggestion was made by the antiquarian Richard Fenton in *Tours in Wales*, ed. Fisher, London, 1917, p.92.

12. Quoted in E. Alfred Jones, "The Welsh Correspondents of John Wilkes", *Cymmrodor*, XXIX, 1919, p.129.

13. In December, 1769, Garrick wrote to Evan Lloyd, "You know I call myself a Welchman", Cardiff City Library, Ms.3.18, ff.37-40.

14. *Memoirs of Thomas Jones, Penkerrig, Radnorshire*, Walpole Society, Vol. 32, London, 1951, p.21.

15. Evan Lloyd to his father, 13 April 1773, NLW Ms.12294, letter 24.

16. *Morning Post*, November 1780.

17. *St James's Chronicle*, 18 August 1763.

18. W.D. Leathart, *The Origin and Progress of the Gwyneddigion Society of London*, London, 1831, p.22.

19. "Fflangell Ysgorpionog i'r Methodistiaid", *Gwaith Prydyddawl y Ddiweddar Rice Jones o'r Blaenau, Meirion*, 1818, p.192.

20. David Garrick, *Private Correspondence*, ed. J. Boaden, London, 1831, ii, 357, quoted in Cecil J. Price, *A Man of Genius and a Welch Man*, Swansea, 1963.

21. Despite the extensive preparations made for his visit, the King was reluctant to come ashore (since he was on his way to Ireland) and had to be prevailed upon

by the Marquis of Anglesey.

22. Onions were occasionally mentioned in the seventeenth-century satires as growing in the Welsh garden, beside the leeks and garlick.

23. *Tours through Wales and Ireland*, 1819, Yale Center for British Art, un-numbered manuscript, signed by "Percy Bull, son of John Bull, shorthand writer to the Houses of Parliament".

IV

1. Thomas Pennant, op. cit., I, p.365. Pennant was criticising a sculpture by Robert Wynne, see Peter Lord, "Life before Wilson", *Gwenllian*, op. cit., p.163.

2. Pennant's descriptions of the circumstances surrounding the production of the prints, quoted through this chapter, are taken from his *Literary Life*, 1793. The Grangerised copy of the *Literary Life*, NLW 12706E, includes the press cuttings and other additional material quoted.

3. Francis Grose, 1731-1791. The extra-illustrated copy in NLW of the *Tours...*, vol.4, has a caricature drawing by Grose of an old woman, presumably done in Wales, p.273.

4. See *The whole of the Proceedings... in the Cause of the King... against the Rev. William Davies Shipley*, 1784, p.107.

5. DNB under Shipley.

6. Dorothy George, "Some Caricatures of the Clergy of Wales", *NLW Journal*, IV, 1945, p.54-5.

7. Clough is untraced. The drawing is NLW PB8171 and if not the original is a very accurate copy.

8. Thomas Sternhold, d.1549, composed metrical versions of the Psalms which he "wished to substitute for the 'obscene' ballads of the court and people", DNB.

9. BL Add.Ms.9850.

10. This may, however, have been George Cruikshank, junior, also a caricaturist. Parry was between the two men in age.

V

1. For an analysis of the image, see Evan J. Jones, "Martial's Epigram on the Happy Life, Simwnt Vychan's Translation; An Interesting Broadside Printed in 1571", *The Bulletin of the Board of Celtic Studies*, vol.3, 1927, p.286-97.

2. Richard Ellis, *An Elizabethan Broadside in the Welsh Language*, Aberystwyth, 1904.

3. For Pitts, see Leslie Shepard, *John Pitts, Ballad Printer of Seven Dials*, Pinner, Middx, 1969. For Catnach, see Charles Hindley, *History of the Catnach Press*, London, 1886.

4. For a detailed discussion of Hughes's relationship with printers in this period, see Peter Lord, *Hugh Hughes*, op. cit..

5. Carey Morris, *Art and Religion in Wales*. W.H. Davies is quoted from his *Poet's Pilgrimage* by Patrick Abercrombie, "Wales: A Study in the Contrast of Country and Town", *Transactions of the Honourable Society of Cymmrodorion*, 1922-3, p.182.

6. Poster printed by Isaac Thomas, NLW, Cardigan Printer's File.

7. See Peter Lord, "The Meaning of the Naive Image", *Gwenllian*, op. cit., p.73.

8. *Slater's Directory* for 1851 gives the name of one engraver in Cardigan, Matthias John Turnor, Pendre, but he does not appear in the census of 1841 or 1851, so presumably his stay was short.

9. For the correspondence about *Oriel y Beirdd*, see Peter Lord, *Y Chwaer-Dduwies*, op. cit., p.23-26.

10. Hugh Humphreys, *The Celebrated Cambrian Linguist, or, the History of Dic Aberdaron*, Caernarfon, 1866, in the appendix written by Robert Ellis, Cynddelw.

11. William Roscoe, *Memoir of Richard Roberts Jones, of Aberdaron*, London, 1822.

12. Mayer's letter is quoted in Peter Lord, *Artisan Painters*, op. cit., p.46, where William Roos's portrait is illustrated, p.7. There are also two fine naive carvings of Dic Aberdaron based on Clements's image. They are illustrated in Peter Lord, *Gwenllian*, op. cit..

VI

1. In his diary, Hugh Hughes records meeting a painter called Harris in Llandeilo, 6 October 1821, NLW Ms.Cwrt Mawr 130A, who was certainly not related to the family of maritime painters of that name active in Swansea a little later.

2. See Paul Joyner, *A Place for a Poussin*, PhD thesis, Cambridge, 1988. Joyner noted 84 references to assorted artists and teachers in Swansea between 1750 and 1850. Second to Swansea came Caernarfon with 27.

3. Dorothy George, "Some caricatures of Wales and Welshmen", *NLW Journal*, V, 1947, no.1, p.10., reported McLean saying in 1830 that the subject of the caricature was "a celebrated whip, who made herself elegantly conspicuous by driving about in a smart chaise and pair with two booted and spurred skipjacks as outriders".

4. For details of the scandal, see Peter Lord, *Hugh Hughes*, op. cit..

5. For a pub sign on the same theme, see Peter Lord, *Artisan Painters*, op. cit., p.15.

6. For responses to Salem, see Peter Lord, "Salem: A National Icon", *Gwenllian*, op. cit..

7. After the death of his father, John Roberts compiled almanacks as "mab y diweddar Robert Roberts" (son of the late Robert Roberts), published by John Jones, Llanrwst. The almanack for 1840 is illustrated with the small key block of Hugh Hughes's *The Landing of His Majesty, King George the Fourth...* Robert Roberts knew Hugh Hughes—he visited his studio in London on 21 June 1826, for instance, an event recorded by William Owen Pughe in his diary, NLW Ms.13248B.

8. Morris Williams, Nicander, 1809-74, had been apprenticed to a carpenter in Llanystumdwy before going to Oxford.

9. John Davies, Gwyneddon, "Llenyddiaeth Newyddiadurol Cymru", *Y Traethodydd*, 1884, p.184.

10. *Carnarvon and Denbigh Herald*, 19 March 1836.

11. For the national costume and the Abergavenny Eisteddfodau, see Peter Lord, *Y Chwaer-Dduwies*, chapter 2.

12. The most that the oppressed could do was to "send their complaints in respectful and humble petitions to their governors." Edward Morgan, *John Elias, Life, Letters and Essays*, 1973, no imprint, p.375.

13. The portraits published in the book are grouped tightly together and only that of Frost is based on an original common to both prints. For Mullock see John Wilson. *James Flewitt and the Victorian Achievement*, Newport, 1993.

14. Hugh Hughes, text to "Dame Venedotia Sousing the Spies", *Pictures for the Million of Wales*, Cardiff, 1848.

15. *Illustrated London News*, 24 June 1843, p.432, and the following quotation.

16. Hugh Hughes, *Y Gynulleidfa*, Carmarthen, 1848, p.6.

17. For the play, see *Brad y Llyfrau Gleision*, ed. Prys Morgan, Llandysul, 1991. For the relationship of the drama to the cartoons, see Peter Lord, "John Gibson and Hugh Hughes", *Gwenllian*, op. cit..

18. NLW Ms. 12021C.

19. NLW Ms. 1889E.

20. Richard Williams Morgan, *Amddiffyniad yr Iaith Gymraeg*, Caernarfon, 1858, p.iv, and following quotation.

21. Ellis's grandfather on his mother's side was John Roberts, Siôn Lléyn.

22. Rose Place was another of the Welsh Methodist chapels in Liverpool.

23. Ellis Wynne, 1671-1734, author of *Gweledigaetheu y Bardd Cwsc*, 1703, considered a classic of Welsh-language prose, but written from an Anglican and royalist standpoint.

24. *North Wales Chronicle*, 5 March 1859.

25. This obscure reference may be to a dispute between Hugh Hughes and William Rees, Gwilym Hiraethog, carried on in an abusive exchange of letters to *Yr Amserau* in 1854-55. Rees responded to Hughes's eccentric views on mission and his attacks on the Ministry with a piece entitled, *Yr Eglwys yn yr Awyr*, (The Church in the Air).

26. Quoted in G.J. Williams, "Ab Ithel", *Y Llenor*, 1933, p.216-30, and 1934, p.88-100.

27. For Haggar and travelling cinemas, see David Berry, *Wales and Cinema*, Cardiff, 1994, section 1, and especially the illustration, p.49.

All pictures in this book are reproduced courtesy of the National Library of Wales, except for the following:
p. 52, 54, 58, 64, 66, 71, 72, 81, 116, courtesy of the British Museum
p.37, 40, 41, 43, 44, by permission of the British Library
p.85 courtesy of the National Museum of Wales
p.12 Powysland Museum, Welshpool
p.21 Yale Center for British Art, New Haven, Ct.
p.3 Hulton Picture Library, London
p.49 Bangor Museum
p.83 Ironbridge Gorge Museum, Elton Collection
p.135 Newport City Museum and Art Gallery
We should like to express our gratitude to all the above institutions.

INDEX

Page numbers in italics indicate that illustrations are included. Order of entries follows the English alphabet

165